EXPLORING

A GUIDED JOURNEY

GOD'S

THROUGH HIS WORD

PROMISES

TERRY ZUEHSOW

CONCORDIA PUBLISHING HOUSE · SAINT LOUIS

Published by Concordia Publishing House
3558 S. Jefferson Ave., St. Louis, MO 63118-3968
1-800-325-3040 • cph.org

Manufactured in the United States of America

1 2 3 4 5 6 7 8 9 10 33 32 31 30 29 28 27 26 25 24

PRAISE FOR *EXPLORING GOD'S PROMISES*

What a blessing it is to see this book in the works. The purpose of *Exploring God's Promises* is to help us apply God's Word to our lives—our joys, our tough times, our every situation. A neat feature of this book is that you can respond personally to the God who knows your name, as Isaiah 43:1 tells us. Please read, enjoy, and take to heart these wonderful messages from God's Word.

Mary Alice Minirth, writer and life coach

This book of assurances is unique and special. It's intensely biblical. You'll hear God speak to you personally—through His Word. However, it also reflects a loving father's deep concern for his daughter. You'll be blessed.

Dr. Gene Getz, pastor; professor; author

God works through His Word. *Exploring God's Promises* embraces this expansive truth, narrows it down to the reader, and connects it to promises God makes in His Word and through His Son, Jesus, the Word made flesh (John 1:14). I believe you will find this book to be profound, for your hope abounds when you know God is at work through His Word; personal, as love for God and others finds expression when it deeply impacts your life; and penetrating, as the laser-like truth of His Word is a solid foundation for your faith and trust in Him in every circumstance of life.

Steve Wagner, pastor, Concordia Lutheran Church, San Antonio, Texas; director, Pastor360

Through insightful reflections, Terry Zuehsow intertwines God's inspired Word and enduring promises with questions that facilitate a deeper engagement with Scripture. Since the heart and emotions can be deceptive, Zuehsow's book guides us to experience healing and renewal by anchoring our trust in God's enduring promises. This book is a valuable resource for those seeking guidance, inspiration, and renewed assurance of God's purpose and unconditional love.

Florene West, director, Our Savior Lutheran Preschool, McKinney, Texas

Has anyone ever written a book just for you? Now you can say that someone has! *Exploring God's Promises* shows Terry's commitment to thoughtful education, helping everyone know God in a deep, meaningful, and personal way. Even though I'm a lifelong Christian, reading Terry's book made me realize what God's promises are, how many there are, and how they belong specifically to me (and you!). He distilled promises from every part of the Bible so that the assurances of God are at your fingertips. Read it and see the wondrous love that God has for you.

Tara M. Niendorf, attorney

Exploring what God has done on my behalf through Terry's book was deeply moving and powerfully humbling. As yesterday, today, and forever promises came to light, my relationship with the everlasting, loving God increased. I even found myself growing in confidence as a child of God as I journaled my feelings. Most assuredly, the Holy Spirit dwelt in my mind, heart, and soul as this gem of writing unfolded itself before me.

Anni Jezek, retired educational coach;
master's degree in educational leadership from Concordia University Texas

---

Exploring God's Promises is a concise and organized study of the promises of God found in every facet of the Bible. Terry Zuehsow prepares his readers with ways to get the most from his book, and space for journaling is included to assist the readers in exploring their relationship with God and considering His promises. Mr. Zuehsow's faith and close relationship with God are evident in his research and illustrations, and he makes God's promises personal to all who study His Word.

Larry Wissner, retired LCMS school administrator

This book is for every Christian who would like to know in a more tangible way the promises of God. *Exploring God's Promises* is helpful, interesting, relatable, compelling, accurate, theologically appropriate, and very moving. Terry takes the reader on a transformative journey through the scriptural promises of God. Sometimes in the storms of life, it is difficult to see that we are not alone or even to realize that anyone cares for us. But through this book, readers can trace the times God has cared deeply for them, comforted them, and enabled them.

Jacqueline Truax, retired international marketing project manager;
graduate marketing studies professor; principal, BSEI

For many years, I traveled on a spiritual pilgrimage, seeking not only the promises of God but also a way to convince myself the promises were actually for me. When I read Terry's book, I found exactly what I was looking for. Drawing on both serious griefs and wonderful triumphs in his life, Terry has carefully searched for God's promises, and he presents them in such a way that readers will be assured that the promises are for them. My journey through these pages has deepened my faith and my love for the Lord, who indeed has promised to meet all our needs.

Karen Brinkmann, senior test development specialist

CONTENTS

ACKNOWLEDGMENTS

What an amazing journey this has been! I joyfully acknowledge my daughter Sara, who, in the midst of deep pain from a shattered relationship and an unexpected journey into single parenthood, desired a personalized collection of God's promises (and didn't know that I was working on one already). She and my other daughter, Kate, have been invaluable in helping me throughout the development of this devotional book.

I am indebted to Joshua Hansard, a brother in Christ who was also healing from a similarly devastating situation. He introduced me to several books about God's ongoing activity in our lives, through which I was inspired to envision this book in its current form. I am thankful for my pastor, David Thompson, who has encouraged me throughout this endeavor, diligently reviewing my work and helping me resolve critical theological issues.

I am thankful for my team of editors, including Kristen E. Clark, Kim Parker Nyman, Rick Nyman, Michael J. Sweeney, and Jamie Moldenhauer. I especially appreciate my beloved wife, Angi, who has been very supportive and has graciously allowed me the time necessary to bring this concept to fruition over several years. She has lovingly assisted me in a careful review of the text and in ensuring the accuracy of the selected Bible verses.

Above all, I humbly and gratefully acknowledge the triune God—Father, Son, and Holy Spirit—who has given us His amazing and excellent promises and assurances. I begin to see how the specific gifts, abilities, and experiences the Lord has provided me over the years have made such a book possible, and I recognize He has guided and enabled me throughout the book's development. God in Christ has demonstrated yet again His power and commitment to work all things together for good for those who love Him and are called according to His purpose.

To God be the glory!

INTRODUCTION

Welcome to the start of a unique journey through the promises of God. Here you will have the opportunity to explore all God has done, is doing, and will do on your behalf. Although the assurances of God presented in the following chapters apply to every believer in Jesus Christ, it is my prayer that you will personalize each promise in your own heart and mind.

In this book, I identify nearly 230 distinct promises and assurances, drawn from almost 1,400 verses throughout the Bible. I continue to be astounded by the absolute consistency of God and His message to us throughout the 66 books of the Bible, written over a period of some fifteen hundred years. By God's grace, I am now seeing Scripture through new lenses—not leading to any new doctrines, but definitely to deeper love and excitement! It is my distinct joy to share those lenses with you.

All quoted Scripture verses are from the English Standard Version of the Bible (ESV) unless otherwise noted. I have used italics to highlight specific promises and assurances within each verse. For clarity, I have replaced key pronouns for God with implied divine names in square brackets, and I have capitalized the remaining divine pronouns. For example, the following promise about you being a citizen of Christ's kingdom looks like this in the ESV:

> **He has delivered us from the domain of darkness and transferred us to the kingdom of his beloved Son.** (COLOSSIANS 1:13)

Here's an example of how it might be formatted in this book:

> **[*The Father*] *has* delivered us from the domain of darkness and *transferred us to the kingdom of His beloved Son.***
> (COLOSSIANS 1:13)

After each of God's promises, you are invited to respond directly to Him through a journaling prompt. I suggest that you journey through this book together with one or more traveling companions, sharing your thoughts and insights with one another along your way.

I pray that the Holy Spirit will open your heart and mind so that God's dependable and powerful Word may have its full effect on you.

EVERY GOOD THING THAT IS IN YOU

The apostle Paul sent a brief letter to his friend Philemon. In it, Paul prayed that Philemon and all those he engaged might gain "the full knowledge of every good thing that is in us for the sake of Christ" (Philemon 6). So what all is included in "every good thing"? Have you ever meditated about all that is now yours as a believer in the Lord Jesus Christ? Have you wondered about God's thoughts concerning you from before the universe began? Have you considered all that changed for you when Jesus Christ died on the cross, arose from the dead, and ascended into heaven for you? How much do you know about God's promises for you day by day, moment by moment during your life here on earth? And what can you confidently look forward to after this life is over?

Several years ago, one of my Bible teachers was considering John 3:16 with us:

> **God so loved the world, that He gave His only Son, that whoever believes in Him should not perish but have eternal life.**

In order to deepen our individual connection with this familiar Bible verse, the teacher suggested that we insert our own names in place of the more general nouns and pronouns. Try that with your name in the blanks:

> **God so loved ______________________________, that He gave His only Son, that ______________________________ should not perish but have eternal life.**

That felt remarkably different to me.

Describe your reaction to reading this Bible verse with your name in it.

READING PAST GOD'S PROMISES

At times, I have tended to gloss over the promises in God's Word and to focus instead on what ***I*** should be doing—trying to keep God's Law. I mistakenly assumed that since God already did so much for me, it was now primarily up to ***me*** to do my best for Him. Whenever I succumb to such thinking, I become less peaceful, more driven, and less loving. I feel the weight of living a "Christian life" squarely on my own shoulders. This typically leaves me feeling either self-righteously proud or woefully inadequate.

Paul very much wanted to help us avoid this trap. He dedicated the entire first half of his letter to the Ephesians exclusively to remarkable facts about

- **yesterday**, what God has already accomplished for you,
- **today**, what God is doing in your life now, and
- **forever**, what God will continue to do for you into eternity.

Paul earnestly prayed that you would realize this and take it fully to heart:

> For this reason, because I have heard of your faith in the Lord Jesus and your love toward all the saints, I do not cease to give thanks for you, remembering you in my prayers, that the God of our Lord Jesus Christ, the Father of glory, may give you the Spirit of wisdom and of revelation in the knowledge of Him, having the eyes of your hearts enlightened, that you may know what is *the hope to which He has called you* [yesterday], what are *the riches*

> *of His glorious inheritance in the saints* [forever], and what is *the immeasurable greatness of His power toward us who believe* [today], according to the working of His great might that He worked in Christ when He raised Him from the dead and seated Him at His right hand in the heavenly places, far above all rule and authority and power and dominion, and above every name that is named, not only in this age but also in the one to come. (EPHESIANS 1:15–21)

FEELING UNLOVABLE

I suspect we all struggle at times, feeling as if God's assurances don't fully apply to us. Sometimes you may feel alone, afraid, unloved, unlovable, abandoned, or hopeless. You may accept that God *has* to love you because of what Christ did, but you are not always sure that He *likes* you very much. Perhaps you see yourself as a second-class Christian, of limited value, usefulness, and significance to God. On occasion, you might even feel like a failure or an embarrassment to Him.

If you experience such feelings, you are actually in good company. Try doing a quick survey of the first few verses of each psalm. In a quarter of them, you will discover many similar feelings and fears expressed passionately. But in these same psalms, you will also find confessions of the reality and certainty of God's assurances and the hope and comfort that they bring—honest feelings met by powerful and rock-solid promises.

HOW GOD REALLY FEELS ABOUT YOU

How does God actually feel about you? He loves you passionately and forever (Jeremiah 31:3)! We learn from the Scriptures that even before creation began, God was thinking about you and chose you to be His own (Ephesians 1:3–6). And He never changes (Malachi 3:6; James 1:17; Hebrews 13:8)!

But why would God populate His perfect universe with people like us, who were free to reject Him? If God knew full well that the people He created would spurn His love, fall into sin, and fundamentally damage His creation, why even go through with it at all? Why didn't He just make us so we *had* to love Him? Think about it. If you *had* to love your parents, spouse, child, or friend, would that really be love?

GOD'S EVERLASTING LOVE FOR YOU

Apparently, it was and is so important to God that you genuinely love Him that He was willing to endure all the sin, evil, and even His Son's death on a cross in order that He might finally achieve an eternal love relationship with you (Hebrews 12:1–2). From the very beginning, Jesus' death and resurrection were part of God's plan to make you holy and to woo you to Himself (1 Peter 1:18–21; Acts 2:23–24). Jesus declared that God's greatest desire is that you "love the Lord your God with all your heart and with all your soul and with all your strength and with all your mind" (Luke 10:27).

The apostle John reminds us that our love for God is only made possible by Him having first loved us (1 John 4:19). Jesus wants you to know that both He and His Father love you as much as they love each other (John 15:9; 17:23)! Imagine how great that love must be! God treasures you (Exodus 19:5), you are precious to Him (Isaiah 43:4), and you are His delight (Isaiah 62:4). He rejoices over you and is glad in you (Isaiah 65:19). Every little detail about you is cherished by Him, from when you were first knit together in your mother's womb (Psalm 139:13) to the day you die to be with Him (Psalm 116:15). He has numbered the hairs on your head (Luke 12:7). Evidently, He even journals about you (Psalm 56:8)!

A TOOL FOR BELIEVERS IN CHRIST

Exploring God's Promises is not intended to replace your Bible reading but rather to serve as a supporting devotional tool. This book does not chronicle God's involvement in history, which reveals much about God's character and confirms the certainty of prophecies yet to be fulfilled. It speaks little about living in a God-pleasing manner, although being grounded in God's assurances makes possible the life of good works, which our Lord created us for in Christ Jesus (Ephesians 2:10). Nor does this book substantially address God's wrath and judgment, hell, or the influence of the devil, the world, and your own sinful nature, although it is only through God's mighty promises that you experience His grace and are empowered to confess your sins, receive God's forgiveness, and ultimately be victorious over evil.

True Christian faith is grounded in the cross of Jesus Christ (Galatians 6:14)—on your dependence upon God for forgiveness and restoration (1 John 1:8–9). Focusing exclusively on God's assurances apart from the full context of His Word might delude some into expecting heaven on earth, a life free today from temptation, sin, disappointment, sorrow, troubles, and persecution. The day is indeed coming when, either through your death or the Lord's return, you will experience such perfection for eternity. Today, however, your Lord reminds you, "In the world you will have tribulation. But take heart; I have overcome the world" (John 16:33). Even in this fallen world, "we know that for those who love God all things work together for good, for those who are called according to His purpose" (Romans 8:28). In the midst of it all, "we are more than conquerors through Him who loved us" (Romans 8:37). Christ's parting words to us before ascending into heaven were, "And behold, I am with you always, to the end of the age" (Matthew 28:20).

INTENDED AUDIENCE

As you've probably surmised, this collection of God's promises and assurances is specifically targeted to *Christians*, who believe in the one true God—Father, Son (Jesus Christ), and Holy Spirit (Matthew 28:19; see also the "Names of God" section at the end of this book). By the power of the Holy Spirit, believers acknowledge and confess their sins and trust in Jesus Christ's atoning sacrifice for them on the cross. The Spirit enables them to grow in their love for God and for all who belong to Him (Galatians 5:22–23). And they are assured of spending eternity together with God and all believers in His glorious kingdom (Revelation 21:3).

Assuming this describes you, an exciting journey through the multifaceted assurances of God awaits you. If you happen to be reading this book but are not a Christian at this time, I pray that what follows will help paint for you a compelling picture of all that God in

Christ has done for you and of His unchanging will to be in a loving relationship with you both now and forever.

WHAT GOD SAYS ABOUT HIS WORD AND HIS PROMISES

God's Word is totally accurate, dependable, and life-transforming. It has been "breathed out" by God Himself (2 Timothy 3:16), and the entirety of His Word is truth (Psalm 119:160; John 17:17). The Word of God accomplishes His purposes (Isaiah 55:11). It is "living and active" (Hebrews 4:12), "at work in you" (1 Thessalonians 2:13), and "profitable for teaching, for reproof, for correction, and for training in righteousness" (2 Timothy 3:16).

Regarding God's promises, the apostle Peter wrote,

> **His divine power has granted to us all things that pertain to life and godliness, through the knowledge of Him who called us to His own glory and excellence, by which He has granted to us His precious and very great promises.** (2 PETER 1:3–4)

These marvelous promises serve as a sure and steadfast anchor for your soul (Hebrews 6:19). Our Lord, who has made these promises to you, is faithful (Hebrews 10:23; Psalm 145:13), and you can be certain that all God's promises find their complete fulfillment in Jesus Christ (2 Corinthians 1:20).

GETTING THE MOST FROM THIS BOOK

Read every quoted Bible verse carefully and deliberately. Examine the verse references whenever you wish, and use them to further explore the sections of Scripture from which individual promises and assurances have been drawn. The related verses that follow point to similar assurances throughout the Bible, highlighting the remarkable consistency of God's Word and allowing you to further explore a particular promise or assurance as God leads you.

Each promise is followed by a journaling prompt—an invitation for you to have a conversation with God about what He is promising you in His Word and how His promise impacts you. In your response to each prompt, consider writing directly to God in Jesus' name, addressing Him as "You" and "Your," while referring to yourself using "I," "me," and "my." This approach can open up space and time for you to more deeply reflect upon what He wants you to know. The Holy Spirit can use such opportunities to help you grow in faith, hope, and love. Feel free to use sentences, phrases, lists, or illustrations.

You are not limited to the prompts; I encourage you to record whatever God's Word inspires in you. Write what you are realizing about God, such as the reality and extent of His love, grace, faithfulness, goodness, holiness, wisdom, and power toward you. Similarly, express how each passage leads you to respond to Him—perhaps in praying for insight and understanding, confessing your sins, acknowledging the faith and hope that is in you, or expressing your love for God through worshiping Him and loving and serving others. Also, include any thoughts and insights from your fellow travelers that resonate with you.

PRAYING FOR YOU

I am praying that God will richly bless your journey of exploring His precious promises and assurances and that your love for Him will continue to grow more and more. Please do not rush through the following pages. Take your time and think deeply about all that is now yours in Christ. You are certainly encouraged to revisit this book as God leads you. And above all, please *do* take it personally!

I invite you to savor Paul's prayer for you found in Ephesians 3:14–21:

> **For this reason I bow my knees before the Father, from whom every family in heaven and on earth is named, that according to the riches of His glory He may grant you to be strengthened with power through His Spirit in your inner being, so that Christ may dwell in your hearts through faith—that you, being rooted and grounded in love, may have strength to comprehend with all the saints what is**

the breadth and length and height and depth, and to know the love of Christ that surpasses knowledge, that you may be filled with all the fullness of God. Now to Him who is able to do far more abundantly than all that we ask or think, according to the power at work within us, to Him be glory in the church and in Christ Jesus throughout all generations, forever and ever. Amen.

YESTERDAY

That you may know what is the hope to which [God] has called you.

EPHESIANS 1:18

"It is finished!" That was Jesus' proclamation to you from the cross. What was finished? That's the focus of this section. Here you can reflect on all that God has already accomplished in and for you through His Son's life, death, and resurrection. Here you are reminded of God's love for you from eternity and of everything that is now true for you in Christ.

This section doesn't focus on things that are happening today or that may happen someday. It's not about what you must do or about levels of holiness you must achieve. It is exclusively about what God Himself has done to break the power and consequences of sin within you. In Christ, God has fully dealt with everything that stood in the way of your perfect love relationship with Him.

If you ever find yourself wondering whether you are good enough to get into heaven, ask yourself what part of Jesus Christ's sacrifice for you was insufficient or inadequate. Since it was complete, just as He declared, you are on very solid ground indeed! You are free to live in total confidence that all of God's yesterday assurances are absolutely true for you, now and always.

GOD FOREKNEW AND PREDESTINED ME

ROMANS 8:29

Do you realize that you have been on God's mind and in His heart from before creation? Your presence at this time in history and in this place is a matter not of chance but of God's deliberate design. In Christ, He has provided you all that you need to live securely, meaningfully, and effectively.

1

Beloved before Time Began

How amazing that God loved you even before the beginning of time! Scripture showcases this ultimate love story, exploring God's timeless, costly, and unchanging love for you. He created the universe and, even before that, He planned the sacrifice of His Son—all for you. He intended for you to have a true love relationship with Him, and it couldn't have been real love if you were not given the ability and freedom to reject Him. He has always loved you, and He has enabled you to love Him.

GOD, YOU WANT ME TO KNOW ABOUT . . .

YOUR *EVERLASTING* LOVE FOR ME

[The Lord says,] "*I have loved you with an everlasting love*; therefore I have continued My faithfulness to you." (JEREMIAH 31:3)

Related verses: Psalm 103:17; John 3:16; Romans 8:37, 39; 2 Thessalonians 2:16; 1 John 3:1; 4:16.

Share with the Lord your reactions to this amazing reality: His love for you predates the world, is in full effect today, and never ends.

GOD, YOU WANT ME TO KNOW ABOUT . . .

YOUR *REDEEMING* LOVE FOR ME

With the Lord there is steadfast love, and with Him is plentiful redemption. (PSALM 130:7)

This is real love—not that we loved God, but that He loved us and sent His Son as a sacrifice to take away our sins. (1 JOHN 4:10 NLT)

Related verses: Isaiah 43:4; 54:10; Jonah 4:2; Micah 7:18; John 3:16; 1 Corinthians 1:30; Galatians 2:20; Ephesians 2:4; Revelation 1:5.

Examine before the Lord God the evidence these verses present of the reality and extent of His love for you.

GOD, YOU WANT ME TO KNOW ABOUT . . .

YOUR *STEADFAST* LOVE FOR ME

As high as the heavens are above the earth, so great is [the Lord's] steadfast love toward those who fear Him. (PSALM 103:11)

Related verses: Exodus 34:6; 1 Chronicles 16:34; Psalm 17:7; 32:10; 40:11; 42:8; 69:16; 103:17; 107:43; 130:7; Hosea 2:19; Micah 7:18; 2 Thessalonians 3:5; 1 John 4:16.

***Steadfast* means "unchanging and faithful." Recall to your Lord some ways in which you have experienced His steadfast love in your life.**

2

Highly Valued

When my parents told others something they appreciated about me, I recall feeling very special and loved. But proud parents who show pictures and share stories about their children have nothing on God! God highly values you, and He describes you in His Word as His treasured possession, His crown of beauty, His delight, and His source of joy. Perhaps you're asking, "Me? Really?" Most definitely!

GOD, YOU WANT ME TO KNOW THAT . . .

YOU HAVE SET YOUR HEART ON ME

What is man, that You make so much of him, and that You set Your heart on him? (JOB 7:17)

Related verses: Deuteronomy 7:13; 32:10; Psalm 56:9; Isaiah 43:4.

Indicate to God Almighty what it means for you to know that He pays attention to you and sets His heart on you.

GOD, YOU WANT ME TO KNOW THAT . . .

I AM YOUR TREASURE

You are a people holy to the LORD your God. The LORD your God has chosen you to be a people for His treasured possession, out of all the peoples who are on the face of the earth. (DEUTERONOMY 7:6)

Related verses: Job 7:17; Isaiah 26:11; 43:4; 62:3; Malachi 3:17.

Identify some things, people, or experiences that you treasure. Ponder before the Lord your God what it means to you that He Himself treasures *you*.

GOD, YOU WANT ME TO KNOW THAT . . .

I AM YOUR DELIGHT

You shall no more be termed Forsaken, and your land shall no more be termed Desolate, but *you shall be called My Delight Is in Her*, and your land Married; *for the LORD delights in you*, and your land shall be married. (ISAIAH 62:4)

Related verses: 2 Samuel 22:20; Psalm 41:11; 44:3; Proverbs 3:12.

Express to the Lord your God why it's amazing that God doesn't just tolerate or put up with you but that He actually *delights* in you.

GOD, YOU WANT ME TO KNOW THAT . . .

I AM YOUR JOY

As the bridegroom rejoices over the bride, so shall your God rejoice over you. (ISAIAH 62:5)

For the joy that was set before Him **[, *Jesus*] endured the cross, despising the shame, and is seated at the right hand of the throne of God.** (HEBREWS 12:2)

Related verses: Numbers 6:25–26; Zephaniah 3:17; Jude 24.

Consider what was the joy that was set before Jesus and how that joy might have actually involved you. Describe to Him your reactions.

3

All in God's Plan

What precious comfort and assurance to know that God elected you in Christ before creation to be His very own! You may wonder how that fits with your ability to freely love God or the fact that not everyone goes to heaven. Paul shares two things to help us with this quandary: God's reasoning is way beyond ours (Romans 11:33), and God is never unjust (Romans 9:14). Apparently, God decided that the good news of His choosing you was much too exciting and important to keep secret!

GOD, YOU WANT ME TO KNOW THAT . . .

YOU KNEW ME IN ADVANCE

Your eyes saw my unformed substance; *in Your book were written, every one of them, the days that were formed for me, when as yet there was none of them.* (PSALM 139:16)

Related verses: Romans 8:29; Titus 1:1–2; 1 Peter 1:1–2.

Convey to your Lord the comfort you find in knowing that God prepared every day of your life and that your existence is not merely a cosmic accident.

GOD, YOU WANT ME TO KNOW THAT . . .

YOU PLANNED FOR ME TO BELONG

In love [God our Father] predestined us for adoption to Himself as sons through Jesus Christ, according to the purpose of His will. (EPHESIANS 1:4–5)

Related verses: Isaiah 43:1; Romans 8:29.

God your Father determined long before your birth that you were to become His child, a member of His family. Declare to Him the confidence you experience in knowing this.

GOD, YOU WANT ME TO KNOW THAT . . .

YOU DESTINED ME TO OBTAIN SALVATION

God has not destined us for wrath, but *to obtain salvation through our Lord Jesus Christ.* (1 THESSALONIANS 5:9)

Related verses: Revelation 13:8; 20:15.

The word *destined* means "planned" or "decided in advance." Here you learn that God Himself destined you to obtain not the wrath that you deserved, but rather salvation through His Son. Reflect on this amazing reality and tell God the Father your reactions.

HE ALSO CALLED ME

ROMANS 8:30

One's vocation, or calling, in life is an important biblical concept (2 Timothy 1:9) that has become part of our everyday language. Who do you suppose is doing the calling? And exactly what has He called you to be and do? You are invited to dive into God's Word and explore!

4

Called by Name

How do you feel when a person you've met only briefly in the past remembers your name and details about your life? Do you feel important and respected? God Himself has called you by name with a call that will never be taken back. He has graciously and earnestly reached out to you. He has called you with the sure hope of salvation into a new and vibrant life in His kingdom. Yes, He most assuredly knows your name!

GOD, YOU WANT ME TO KNOW THAT . . .

YOU CALLED ME *PERSONALLY*

Thus says the LORD, . . . "Fear not, for I have redeemed you; *I have called you by name, you are Mine.*" (ISAIAH 43:1)

Related verses: Isaiah 42:6; Matthew 9:13; Romans 8:28; 1 Corinthians 1:24; Ephesians 1:18; 2 Thessalonians 2:14; 2 Timothy 1:9; Revelation 17:14.

We know that the Lord God, King of the universe, calls everyone through His Word. But share with Him what it means to you to realize that He has personally called you by name.

GOD, YOU WANT ME TO KNOW THAT . . .

YOU CALLED ME *PROACTIVELY*

You shall be called Sought Out, A City Not Forsaken. (ISAIAH 62:12)

Related verses: Matthew 13:44–46; Luke 1:68; 19:10; 2 Thessalonians 2:14; 1 Peter 1:20; 3:18.

Visualize what it means that your Lord actually sought you out and pursued you. Present your thoughts to Him.

GOD, YOU WANT ME TO KNOW THAT . . .

YOU CALLED ME *PURPOSEFULLY*

We know that for *those who love God* all things work together for good, for those who *are called according to His purpose.* (ROMANS 8:28)

Related verses: Isaiah 42:6; 1 Corinthians 1:2; Ephesians 2:10; 1 Thessalonians 2:12; 4:7; 2 Timothy 1:9; Hebrews 3:1.

Explore with God the fact that He not only called you as His own but also planned a meaningful and purposeful life for you.

5

Chosen

Have you ever attended a renewal of wedding vows? One spouse might look into the other's eyes and say, "If I had it all to do over, I would still choose you!" How would you feel if those words were directed to you? Honored? Special? Loved? Even though God is fully aware of your faults and shortcomings, He renews His vows to you daily! You did not choose Him, but He has freely chosen you to be His own. He has chosen you to grow in grace, in faith, and in love. Are you feeling special yet?

GOD, YOU WANT ME TO KNOW THAT . . .

YOU CHOSE ME FOR YOURSELF

[God our Father] chose us in [Christ] before the foundation of the world. (EPHESIANS 1:4)

Related verses: Leviticus 20:26; Deuteronomy 7:6–7; Psalm 4:3; 65:4; Isaiah 41:9; Colossians 3:12; 2 Thessalonians 2:13; James 2:5; 1 Peter 2:9; Revelation 17:14.

As a child, did you ever hope to be picked by a neighborhood or playground team captain? Tell God your Father what it means that you were chosen by Him before creation.

GOD, YOU WANT ME TO KNOW THAT . . .

YOU CHOSE MY HERITAGE FOR ME

The Lord, the Most High, . . . chose our heritage for us. (PSALM 47:2, 4)

You have given me the heritage of those who fear Your name. (PSALM 61:5)

Related verses: Psalm 37:18; 127:3; Isaiah 54:17; 58:14.

Your heritage generally consists of possessions or traditions that have been handed down to you from past generations. Your heritage as a believer can include the Bible and Bible-based writings, Christian organizations and roles, sacred music and worship forms, art expressions, and so much more. Recall and thank the Lord, the Most High, for aspects of your heritage in Christ that are especially significant to you.

6

Fearfully and Wonderfully Made

You know that God created the universe and everything in it, but perhaps sometimes you might forget that He specially designed and formed *you*—cell by cell, with your unique DNA, mind, heart, and soul. "Fearfully and wonderfully made" indicates that you were handcrafted by God with great care and attention in a distinct and marvelous way. He made you *exactly* as He intended. You are His masterpiece. Though it is clouded by sin, you still bear the image of your Father in heaven. You are rational, creative, and purposeful. He has high hopes and big plans for you, all leading to His glory and to your perfect joy.

GOD, YOU WANT ME TO KNOW THAT . . .

YOU CREATED ME

You formed my inward parts; You knitted me together in my mother's womb. I praise You, for I am fearfully and wonderfully made. Wonderful are Your works; my soul knows it very well. (PSALM 139:13–14)

Related verses: Job 12:10; 35:10; Psalm 119:73; Proverbs 16:4; Isaiah 44:21; 64:8; Jeremiah 38:16; Zechariah 12:1; Malachi 2:10; Acts 17:28; 1 Corinthians 8:6.

The value of a work of art is often tied to the master who created it. Contemplate before the Lord what it means for you to be His very own unique masterpiece—fearfully and wonderfully made.

GOD, YOU WANT ME TO KNOW THAT . . .

YOU MADE ME IN YOUR IMAGE

God created man in His own image, in the image of God He created him. (GENESIS 1:27)

Related verses: Genesis 1:26, 28; 9:6.

As one uniquely created by God, consider with Him how you have been lovingly designed to display His image to those around you.

7

God Dwells in Me

Augustine, Bishop of Hippo, had been living in a wild, worldly manner for much of his life, until God brought him to faith. Around AD 400, he wrote, "You have made us for Yourself, O Lord, and our hearts are restless until they rest in You." In 1670, Blaise Pascal spoke similarly of an "infinite abyss" inside us, which "can only be filled . . . by God Himself." While people may strive for peace and fulfillment through a variety of things and experiences, you have the one true God—Father, Son, and Holy Spirit—living in you.

GOD, YOU WANT ME TO KNOW THAT . . .

YOU ARE IN ME

Whoever confesses that Jesus is the Son of God, *God abides in him*, and he in God. (1 JOHN 4:15)

Little children, you are from God and have overcome [those prophesying falsely in the spirit of the antichrist], for *He who is in you* is greater than he who is in the world. (1 JOHN 4:4)

Related verses: Exodus 29:45–46; Leviticus 26:11–12; Numbers 35:34; Isaiah 57:15; Zechariah 2:10–11; John 14:23; 1 John 3:24; 4:13, 16.

GOD, YOU WANT ME TO KNOW THAT . . .

YOUR SON IS IN ME

[Jesus said,] "In that day *you will know that I am* in My Father, and you in Me, and I *in you.*" (JOHN 14:20)

To them God chose to make known how great among the Gentiles are the riches of the glory of this mystery, which is *Christ in you*, the hope of glory. (COLOSSIANS 1:27)

Related verses: John 6:56; 14:23; 15:5; Romans 8:10; 1 Corinthians 6:17; 2 Corinthians 13:5; Galatians 2:20; Ephesians 3:17; Colossians 2:9–10; Hebrews 3:14.

GOD, YOU WANT ME TO KNOW THAT . . .

YOUR SPIRIT IS IN ME

By *the Holy Spirit who dwells within us*, guard the good deposit entrusted to you. (2 TIMOTHY 1:14)

Related verses: Isaiah 63:11; Ezekiel 36:27; John 14:16; Acts 2:17–18; Romans 8:9; 1 Corinthians 3:16; Galatians 3:2; Titus 3:6; 1 John 2:20, 27.

Share with God what it means to you that He—Father, Son, and Holy Spirit—is present inside you.

8

Given the Gift of Faith

What exactly is faith? Is it agreement with a set of propositions or doctrines? That is certainly part of faith, but real faith runs much deeper than that. When my first daughter was very young, I took her up with me to see our attic. As I walked down the attic stairs ahead of her, they broke. I landed safely on the floor below, but my daughter, now alone in the attic, looked anxiously to me for help. I held out my arms and said, "Jump, I'll catch you!" Without hesitation, she popped right out of the attic and into my arms. I realized that I had just witnessed a powerful example of genuine faith. She trusted me implicitly that I wouldn't let her fall. That is the kind of faith God produces in you by the mighty working of the Holy Spirit through His Word.

GOD, YOU WANT ME TO KNOW THAT . . .

YOU BROUGHT ME TO FAITH

Let us run with endurance the race that is set before us, looking to *Jesus, the founder and perfecter of our faith.* (HEBREWS 12:1–2)

Related verses: Isaiah 9:2; Romans 5:2; James 2:5; 1 Peter 1:20–21; 1 John 5:20.

Convey to your Lord Jesus Christ the comfort you find in knowing that your faith has been created and is being sustained by Him.

GOD, YOU WANT ME TO KNOW THAT . . .

YOU FULLY ASSURE ME

Let us draw near with a true heart *in full assurance of faith*, with our hearts sprinkled clean from an evil conscience and our bodies washed with pure water. (HEBREWS 10:22)

Related verses: Jeremiah 24:7; Ezekiel 20:44; Philippians 3:10; Hebrews 10:19; 2 Peter 1:1; 1 John 5:13.

Express to God what His phrase "full assurance of faith" means to you and what you have been fully assured of.

GOD, YOU WANT ME TO KNOW THAT . . .

YOU NEVER FORGET ME

[The Lord says,] "Can a woman forget her nursing child, that she should have no compassion on the son of her womb? Even these may forget, yet *I will not forget you. Behold, I have engraved you on the palms of My hands*." (ISAIAH 49:15–16)

Related verses: Deuteronomy 4:31; Isaiah 44:21; Luke 12:8; Revelation 3:5.

Describe to your Lord the security you find in knowing that He has engraved you on His palms.

9

Made Christ's Own

The ultimate put-down might well be "You don't belong here." Few phrases have such power to wound you to the core. Comedian Groucho Marx once quipped that he would never join a club that would accept him as a member. Do you ever feel that way about your membership in Jesus' church? How could a holy God ever include *you* in His club? The amazing fact is that God created the universe and planned the sacrifice of His Son just so that you could belong as an honored member in good standing. You have been baptized into Christ Jesus, into His death and His resurrection, and now everything that is His has become yours! May you thoroughly enjoy your lifetime (and beyond) membership!

GOD, YOU WANT ME TO KNOW THAT . . .

I BELONG TO YOU

Know that the LORD, He is God! It is He who made us, and *we are His; we are His people, and the sheep of His pasture.* (PSALM 100:3)

Not that I have already obtained this or am already perfect, but I press on to make it my own, because *Christ Jesus has made me His own.* (PHILIPPIANS 3:12)

Related verses: Deuteronomy 27:9; 32:9; 1 Samuel 12:22; 1 Chronicles 29:11; Psalm 79:13; Isaiah 44:5; Malachi 3:17; Acts 15:17–18; Romans 1:6; 1 Corinthians 3:23; 6:19–20; 2 Timothy 2:19; 1 Peter 2:9.

The idea of belonging to someone else can clash with your natural desire to do whatever you want to do and to answer to no one. Ponder with your Lord Jesus Christ what it means that you are His person and not your own and why this is truly wonderful news.

GOD, YOU WANT ME TO KNOW THAT . . .

I HAVE BEEN BAPTIZED INTO YOUR SON

As many of you as were baptized into Christ have put on Christ. (GALATIANS 3:27)

Related verses: Matthew 28:19; Romans 6:3–5; 1 Peter 3:21.

Review both the quoted and related verses above. Reflect with Jesus Christ on what it means to you that you have been baptized into Him.

GOD, YOU WANT ME TO KNOW THAT . . .

I AM IN YOUR SON

***Because of* [*God*] *you are in Christ Jesus*, who became to us wisdom from God, righteousness and sanctification and redemption.** (1 CORINTHIANS 1:30)

Related verses: Romans 8:1; 2 Corinthians 1:1; 5:17; Hebrews 3:14; 1 Peter 5:14; 1 John 2:24; 5:20.

What an amazing place to be! Use this Bible verse as a springboard into several things that are true and possible for you now that you find yourself *in Christ*. Thank God for placing you there.

10

Adopted into God's Family

Welcome to the family! What a gracious expression of inclusion and honor! Your relationship with God—Father, Son, and Holy Spirit—is far deeper and richer than any human analogy could ever express. But in His Word, God compares your relationship with Him to that of a child, a brother or sister, an heir, and a lover. All of these roles provide helpful insights into the most amazing relationship since creation: the Father and His Son, Jesus, love you just as much as they love each other!

GOD, YOU WANT ME TO KNOW THAT . . .

YOU ADOPTED ME AS YOUR CHILD

You did not receive the spirit of slavery to fall back into fear, but *you have received the Spirit of adoption as sons, by whom we cry, "Abba! Father!" The Spirit Himself bears witness with our spirit that we are children of God.* (ROMANS 8:15–16)

Related verses: Luke 6:35; John 1:12; Acts 17:28; Romans 8:14; 9:26; 2 Corinthians 6:18; Galatians 4:4–5, 7; Ephesians 1:5; 1 John 3:1–2.

Let your heavenly Father know the significance of Him adopting you.

GOD, YOU WANT ME TO KNOW THAT . . .

YOU ARE MY FATHER

I will be a father to you, and you shall be sons and daughters to Me, says the Lord Almighty. (2 CORINTHIANS 6:18)

Because you are sons, God has sent the Spirit of His Son into our hearts, crying, "Abba! Father!" (GALATIANS 4:6)

Related verses: Isaiah 64:8; Matthew 5:16; 6:4, 9, 14; 7:11; Luke 12:32; Romans 8:15; 2 Corinthians 1:3; Galatians 1:4; Philippians 1:2; 4:20; 1 John 3:1.

✎ *Abba* is an endearing Aramaic term for father—one of an infant's first words, like *dada*. What a surprisingly familiar word with which to address our heavenly Father! Tell your heavenly Abba what it means to you to be His child.

GOD, YOU WANT ME TO KNOW THAT . . .

YOUR SON IS MY BROTHER

[*Jesus*] who sanctifies and those who are sanctified all have one source. That is why He *is not ashamed to call them brothers.* (HEBREWS 2:11)

Related verses: Matthew 12:50; Hebrews 2:13, 17.

✎ Share with Jesus your reaction to this fact: He is proud to be your brother.

GOD, YOU WANT ME TO KNOW THAT . . .

WE'RE ENGAGED TO YOU

[The Lord declares,] "I will betroth you to Me forever. I will betroth you to Me in righteousness and in justice, in steadfast love and in mercy. I will betroth you to Me in faithfulness." (HOSEA 2:19–20)

Related verses: Isaiah 54:5; Hosea 2:16; 2 Corinthians 11:2.

In Bible times, engagement carried the same weight as marriage. As you look forward to the church becoming Christ's Bride in the life to come, explore with the Lord the fact that we are now collectively engaged to Him.

GOD, YOU WANT ME TO KNOW THAT . . .

I'M YOUR PROMISED HEIR

The Spirit Himself bears witness with our spirit that we are children of God, and if children, then heirs—heirs of God and fellow heirs with Christ. (ROMANS 8:16–17)

Related verses: Mark 10:14; Romans 4:13; Galatians 4:7, 28; Ephesians 1:11; Colossians 1:12; James 2:5.

Share what it means to you as God's heir that your inheritance has already been secured. Describe to Him what especially excites you about this inheritance.

11

Assigned Special Roles

As a child of God, you are provided many special and significant roles here on earth and beyond. You did not earn these, but you received them as a part of God's gracious gift to you. He made you a member, or part, of His Body—the fellowship of all believers. You are like a sheep under the Good Shepherd, guarded and guided by our Lord. God declared you His priest, tasked with sharing His love and message with believers and nonbelievers alike. He has planted you in this specific time and place to accomplish His gracious purposes and to extend His love. In all these roles, you are richly blessed, even as God blesses others through you.

GOD, YOU WANT ME TO KNOW THAT . . .

I'M A MEMBER OF CHRIST'S BODY

Now you are the body of Christ and individually members of it. (1 CORINTHIANS 12:27)

Related verses: Luke 18:29–30; 1 Corinthians 1:2; 12:13; 2 Corinthians 1:21; 1 John 1:7.

Thank Jesus Christ for making you a part of His Body on earth, His church, and for surrounding you with fellow believers who love Him and you.

GOD, YOU WANT ME TO KNOW THAT . . .

I'M A SHEEP OF THE GOOD SHEPHERD

You are My sheep, human sheep of My pasture, and I am your God, declares the Lord GOD. (EZEKIEL 34:31)

[Jesus said,] "I am the good shepherd. The good shepherd lays down His life for the sheep." (JOHN 10:11)

Related verses: Psalm 23:1; 74:1; 78:52; 79:13; 95:7; Ezekiel 34:2–3, 5–6, 8, 10–12, 15, 19, 23; Micah 2:12; Matthew 2:6; John 10:2–4, 7–8, 14–15, 27; 21:16–17; Hebrews 13:20.

As a "human sheep" in the Good Shepherd's pasture, review Psalm 23. Indicate to your Good Shepherd reasons why you are thankful for being numbered among His sheep.

GOD, YOU WANT ME TO KNOW THAT . . .

I'M A CITIZEN OF CHRIST'S KINGDOM

[The Father] has delivered us from the domain of darkness and transferred us to the kingdom of His beloved Son. (COLOSSIANS 1:13)

Related verses: Exodus 19:6; Deuteronomy 32:9; Psalm 33:12; Isaiah 33:22; Zechariah 2:12; Revelation 1:6; 5:10.

Consider with the Father the significance of being a subject of Christ the King and a citizen of His kingdom.

GOD, YOU WANT ME TO KNOW THAT . . .

I'M YOUR PRIEST

To [Jesus Christ] who loves us and has freed us from our sins by His blood, and *has made us to be a kingdom and priests to serve His God and Father*—to Him be glory and power for ever and ever! Amen. (REVELATION 1:5–6 NIV)

Related verses: Exodus 19:6; 1 Peter 2:9; Revelation 5:10.

The historic role of priests included being God's ambassadors and praying for others. Summarize for God your Father ways in which you are called to serve as His priest to others today.

GOD, YOU WANT ME TO KNOW THAT . . .

YOU HAVE PLANTED ME IN YOUR FIELD

[The Lord declares,] "I will sow [My people] for Myself in the land." (HOSEA 2:23)

The righteous flourish like the palm tree and grow like a cedar in Lebanon. They are planted in the house of the Lord; they flourish in the courts of our God. (PSALM 92:12–13)

Related verses: Psalm 80:8, 15; 92:14; Isaiah 5:1–2; 27:2; Jeremiah 2:21; 11:17; 17:8; Ezekiel 19:10; Matthew 15:13; 1 Corinthians 3:9.

Contemplate before the Lord your God how purposefully and masterfully He has planted you in this place and time.

HE ALSO JUSTIFIED ME

ROMANS 8:30

The elephant in the room is that your God is perfect, but you are not. He can't tolerate sin, and you can't steer clear of it. These sound like irreconcilable differences, but thankfully, the story does not end there. The same God who called you also took it upon Himself to justify you, which means He made you righteous before Him, just as if you had never sinned. This section explores all that went into your justification.

12

Received the Gift of God's Son

Jesus—a gift unlike any other! Only one thing stood in the way of God's desire for you to dwell with Him in love forever: your sin. God is holy, and He cannot coexist with sin or evil. Only perfect, sinless people can be a part of His kingdom. What you never could have done, God Himself did for you by sending Jesus to take upon Himself the punishment you deserved. The wages of your sin was death, both in time and eternity, but Jesus took your place. What an incredible gift at such a horrific price!

GOD, YOU WANT ME TO KNOW THAT . . .

YOU GAVE ME YOUR SON, JESUS

***God so loved the world, that He gave His only Son,* that whoever believes in Him should not perish but have eternal life.** (JOHN 3:16)

Related verses: Isaiah 9:6; Jeremiah 30:9; Romans 8:32; Galatians 1:4; 4:4–5.

Reflect with God about the astonishing and completely undeserved gift He gave you in the form of His Son, Jesus Christ.

GOD, YOU WANT ME TO KNOW THAT . . .

HE TOOK MY SIN

All we like sheep have gone astray; we have turned—every one—to his own way; and *the Lord has laid on [the Christ] the iniquity of us all.* (ISAIAH 53:6)

For our sake [God] made [Christ] to be sin who knew no sin, so that in Him we might become the righteousness of God. (2 CORINTHIANS 5:21)

Related verses: Psalm 78:38; Isaiah 53:5, 8; Romans 8:3–4; Colossians 2:13–14; 1 Peter 2:24.

Sin literally means "to miss the mark"—breaking God's perfect commandments. Several terms for sin appear in the Bible: ***Trespasses*** involve crossing the line to operate outside of God's will, whether intentionally or not. ***Transgressions*** are deliberate, premeditated trespasses. ***Iniquities*** are more about moving the mark or changing the lines—redefining God's Law to one's own self-justification. You have sinned against God repeatedly in all these ways, but His Son, Jesus Christ, freely accepted all of your sins upon Himself. Describe to the Lord God what this means to you.

GOD, YOU WANT ME TO KNOW THAT . . .

HE SUFFERED AND DIED FOR ME

God shows His love for us in that while we were still sinners, *Christ died for us.* (ROMANS 5:8)

But we see Him who for a little while was made lower than the angels, namely *Jesus, crowned with glory and honor because of the suffering of death, so that by the grace of God He might taste death for everyone.* (HEBREWS 2:9)

Related verses: Isaiah 53:4–5, 8; John 10:11; 11:50–51; Romans 5:6; 14:15; 2 Corinthians 5:14–15; 1 Thessalonians 5:10; Hebrews 12:2; 1 Peter 2:21; 3:18.

You deserved to die eternally. Meditate deeply before Jesus Christ about what it means that He willingly died for you.

GOD, YOU WANT ME TO KNOW THAT . . .

HE ENSURED THE DEVIL'S DESTRUCTION

Since therefore [God's] children share in flesh and blood, [Jesus] Himself likewise partook of the same things, that through death He might destroy the one who has the power of death, that is, the devil. (HEBREWS 2:14)

The reason the Son of God appeared was to destroy the works of the devil. (1 JOHN 3:8)

Related verses: Genesis 3:15; Matthew 16:16–18; Luke 10:18; John 12:31; 16:11; Colossians 2:15; Revelation 12:7–10.

The devil is wicked, powerful, deceitful, and extremely cunning. He bitterly hates God and wants to destroy you. Consider what your chances would have been in defeating him on your own. Express your thanks to Jesus for His decisive victory over the devil through His death and resurrection. Acknowledge to Him that His victory frees you from the devil's power and, when He returns, guarantees the complete destruction of both the devil and his works.

13

Christ Sacrificed Himself

Unlucky number 13? Can you picture the devil and his cohorts gleefully presuming Jesus to be extremely unlucky as He was being nailed to the cross? But in the most incredible turnaround in history, death could not hold Jesus, and His death ended up paying in full everything that you owed. The Jewish Passover celebration, with its annual sacrifice of a spotless lamb and sprinkled blood, found its complete, once-for-all fulfillment in the astounding self-sacrifice of the spotless Lamb of God for you. Jesus' sacrifice of Himself served as the perfect and complete payment for all of your sins before God, His Father.

GOD, YOU WANT ME TO KNOW THAT . . .

YOUR SON IS MY PRIEST AND MY SACRIFICE

Therefore, it was necessary for [Jesus] to be made in every respect like us, His brothers and sisters, *so that He could be our merciful and faithful High Priest before God. Then He could offer a sacrifice that would take away the sins of the people.* (HEBREWS 2:17 NLT)

[Christ] has no need, like those high priests, to offer sacrifices daily, first for His own sins and then for those of the people, since He did this once for all when He *offered up Himself.* (HEBREWS 7:27)

Related verses: John 11:50–51; Romans 3:24–25; 4:25; 1 Corinthians 15:3; Hebrews 4:14–15; 7:26; 10:21; 1 John 3:16; 4:10.

Human priests served as intermediaries between God and His people, helping His people connect to Him while shielding them from His holiness. Priests offered daily sacrifices to God for sins—for their own sins and for the sins of others. Explain to Jesus, your merciful and faithful High Priest, what it means to you that He sacrificed Himself for you, pleads for you before His Father, and has opened up for you free access to God.

GOD, YOU WANT ME TO KNOW THAT . . .

I'M CLEANSED BY HIS BLOOD

[Jesus] took a cup, and when He had given thanks He gave it to them, saying, "Drink of it, all of you, for *this is My blood of the covenant, which is poured out for many for the forgiveness of sins.*" (MATTHEW 26:27–28)

But if we walk in the light, as [God] is in the light, we have fellowship with one another, and *the blood of Jesus His Son cleanses us from all sin.* (1 JOHN 1:7)

Related verses: Leviticus 17:11; Romans 5:9; 1 Corinthians 11:25; Hebrews 9:22; 10:29; 13:12; 1 Peter 1:2; Revelation 1:5.

Being cleansed by someone's blood is an extremely disturbing image, to be sure. But given that the wages of your sin were rightfully eternal death and damnation, recognize before your Lord Jesus the beauty and grace you can find in His astonishing act of love.

GOD, YOU WANT ME TO KNOW THAT . . .

HIS BODY WAS GIVEN FOR ME

[Jesus] took bread, and when He had given thanks, He broke it and gave it to them, saying, "*This is My body, which is given for you.* Do this in remembrance of Me." (LUKE 22:19)

[Christ] Himself bore our sins in His body on the tree, that we might die to sin and live to righteousness. By His wounds you have been healed. (1 PETER 2:24)

Related verses: Isaiah 53:5; 1 Corinthians 11:24; Hebrews 10:19–20.

Jesus Christ, the sinless Son of God, endured an excruciating death on the cross and separation from His Father so you wouldn't have to face the dreadful consequences of your sins. Tell Jesus how participating in His Supper helps keep these amazing facts in your central focus.

GOD, YOU WANT ME TO KNOW THAT . . .

HE DID THIS ONCE FOR ALL

But now, once for all time, [Christ] has appeared at the end of the age to remove sin by His own death as a sacrifice. (HEBREWS 9:26 NLT)

Related verses: Hebrews 2:9; 9:28; 10:10, 14; 1 Peter 3:18.

Even though you sin every day, consider with Jesus Christ how reassuring it is for you to know that His death two millennia ago covers *all* your sin—past, present, and future.

14

Saved by Grace through Faith

At a friend's wedding, his bride's mind went blank when she was to recite her vows. When he softly prompted her, "Love me and serve me," she replied out loud, "Love me and serve me." In the end, she hadn't actually promised him anything! In a sense, your vows to God are much like that. The forces of darkness—the devil, the evil world, and your sinful nature—are more powerful than you yourself could possibly overcome. And on your own, you would never be able to escape God's righteous wrath over your sin. But thanks be to God, who sent His only Son, Jesus Christ, to do for you what you could never have done! You can't guarantee to God how loving and faithful *you* will be, but instead, you can thank *Him* for His incredible gift of grace and declare to Him how loving and faithful *He* is. Be assured that He will take it from there.

GOD, YOU WANT ME TO KNOW THAT . . .

YOU SAVED ME THROUGH FAITH IN YOUR SON

They said, "Believe in the Lord Jesus, and you will be saved, you and your household." (ACTS 16:31)

Related verses: Jeremiah 33:14–16; Luke 2:11; John 3:16–17; Acts 4:12; Romans 5:10; 10:9–10, 13; 1 Corinthians 15:57; 1 Thessalonians 5:9–10; 1 Timothy 1:15; Titus 3:5–6.

Some religions require that you first clean up your act or ensure that your total good deeds outweigh your bad ones before you can start your journey with God. Others call for some form of personal achievement or mastery in order to be acceptable to God. According to this verse, however, what does God actually require of you to be saved? Reflect with

Him on why this requirement is so amazing and wonderful to you.

GOD, YOU WANT ME TO KNOW THAT . . .

YOU DELIVERED ME FROM THE DOMAIN OF DARKNESS

[*The Father*] *has delivered us from the domain of darkness* and transferred us to the kingdom of His beloved Son. (COLOSSIANS 1:13)

Related verses: Psalm 116:8; Galatians 1:3–4.

Recall examples of spiritual darkness you have encountered in this world, as well as instances when God's light has broken through. Express your gratitude to the Father for delivering you from this darkness.

GOD, YOU WANT ME TO KNOW THAT . . .

YOU HAVE GIFTED ME WITH GRACE

The free gift is not like the trespass. For if many died through one man's trespass, much more have *the grace of God and the free gift by the grace of that one man Jesus Christ abounded for many.* (ROMANS 5:15)

Related verses: Acts 15:11; Ephesians 2:8–9; 2 Timothy 1:9; Titus 2:11.

Well, you must have contributed ***something*** to the favorable condition in which you now happily find yourself, right? Based on this verse, comment to God about such sentiment.

GOD, YOU WANT ME TO KNOW THAT . . .

YOU HAVE ACCOMPLISHED THESE IN ME BY YOUR WORD

Of [God's] own will He brought us forth by the word of truth. (JAMES 1:18)

I am not ashamed of *the gospel, for it is the power of God for salvation to everyone who believes,* to the Jew first and also to the Greek. (ROMANS 1:16)

Related verses: Psalm 119:93; Luke 1:77; 1 Corinthians 1:18; James 1:21.

God's Word is the incredibly powerful tool that He used to graciously save you from sin, death, and the devil's power and to make you His own. Consider composing a headline and opening paragraph for a front-page story about this astoundingly Good News (that is, this Gospel). Share with God what His Gospel means to you.

15

Forgiven

You've probably watched a movie or two in which a "not guilty" verdict left people cheering and hugging. Perhaps you have even experienced something like this in real life. With God as your judge and Jesus as your defense attorney, your acquittal is certain. God truly forgives you in Christ and forgets your sins. And there is a lot of cheering and hugging in heaven every time another sinner repents and is declared not guilty (see Luke 15:7).

GOD, YOU WANT ME TO KNOW THAT . . .

YOU HAVE COMPASSION ON ME

***As a father shows compassion to his children, so the LORD shows compassion to those who fear Him.* For He knows our frame; He remembers that we are dust.** (PSALM 103:13–14)

Related verses: Psalm 78:38; Isaiah 54:8, 10; 55:7; Micah 7:19.

Recall with the Lord how you have personally experienced His compassion.

GOD, YOU WANT ME TO KNOW THAT . . .

YOU HAVE SHOWN MERCY TO ME

As for You, O Lord, You will not restrain Your mercy from me. (PSALM 40:11)

Related verses: Exodus 34:6; Deuteronomy 4:31; Isaiah 30:18; Hosea 2:1, 23; Matthew 5:7; Luke 1:50; 6:35–36; 1 Peter 2:10; 2 John 3; Jude 21.

When convicted of a crime, one is likely to beg for mercy rather than justice. Glorify the Lord now for His undeserved mercy to you.

GOD, YOU WANT ME TO KNOW THAT . . .

YOU HAVE ENABLED ME TO REPENT

They glorified God, saying, "Then to the Gentiles also God has granted repentance that leads to life." (ACTS 11:18)

Related verses: Acts 5:31; Romans 2:4; 2 Timothy 2:25.

Submission to God, with genuine remorse for sin and a sincere desire to be changed, does not come naturally. You could not have done it by yourself. Let God know how crucial it is that He Himself has graciously granted repentance to you.

GOD, YOU WANT ME TO KNOW THAT . . .

YOU HAVE FORGIVEN MY SINS

To [Jesus of Nazareth] all the prophets bear witness that *everyone who believes in Him receives forgiveness of sins through His name.* (ACTS 10:43)

Related verses: Psalm 78:38; 85:2; 103:10; Jeremiah 31:34; Ezekiel 20:44; Micah 7:18; Matthew 1:21; 26:28; Luke 1:77; Ephesians 1:7; Colossians 1:14; 1 John 2:12.

You have likely experienced the personal healing and restoration that can result when people genuinely forgive one another. Convey to Jesus what it means to you that all of your sins have been forgiven through His name and how exceedingly important that is to you.

GOD, YOU WANT ME TO KNOW THAT . . .

YOU HAVE FORGOTTEN MY SINS

[The Lord declares,] "I will be merciful toward their iniquities, and *I will remember their sins no more.*" (HEBREWS 8:12)

[God] will again have compassion on us; *He will tread our iniquities underfoot. You will cast all our sins into the depths of the sea.* (MICAH 7:19)

As far as the east is from the west, so far does [the Lord] remove our transgressions from us. (PSALM 103:12)

Related verses: Psalm 85:2; Isaiah 43:25; Jeremiah 31:34.

You may forgive someone who hurt you, but you are unlikely to forget what happened. Indicate to the Lord God how He is different and what that means to you.

16

Redeemed by God

Perhaps you have heard the tale of a boy who builds his own toy boat only to lose it to a sudden river surge. Weeks later, he finds his boat for sale in a resale shop. He does extra work for people until he has enough money to buy his boat back. He then declares the boat "twice his." With God, you are likewise twice His—first created by Him and later redeemed (bought back) by Him. You have been redeemed from your sins and from the curse of the Law (eternal death), and now you are fully forgiven. God paid an exorbitant price to get you back at all costs.

GOD, YOU WANT ME TO KNOW THAT . . .

YOUR SON HAS REDEEMED ME

***I know that my Redeemer lives*, and at the last He will stand upon the earth.** (JOB 19:25)

Christ redeemed us from the curse of the law by becoming a curse for us. (GALATIANS 3:13)

Related verses: Exodus 15:13; 1 Chronicles 17:21; Psalm 111:9; 130:7; Isaiah 44:23–24; 49:26; 62:12; Romans 3:24; Ephesians 1:7.

In Old Testament times, a kinsman-redeemer was a person who delivered or rescued a close relative who was in need. Thank and praise your Lord Jesus Christ for redeeming you from the devil's claim on your life, your slavery to sin, and the deadly curse of the Law.

GOD, YOU WANT ME TO KNOW THAT . . .

HE HAS RANSOMED ME

The Son of Man came not to be served but to serve, and *to give His life as a ransom for many.* (MATTHEW 20:28)

Related verses: Exodus 15:16; Isaiah 35:10; 51:11; Mark 10:45; 1 Corinthians 6:20; 7:23; 1 Timothy 2:6; 1 Peter 1:18–19; Revelation 5:9.

A ransom is the price paid by a redeemer to free a hostage. Consider the extensive ransom Jesus paid to get you back. He had to leave His glory in heaven to be born as a helpless baby. He had to endure all the challenges of life on earth and face the rejection and wickedness of people. He would finally be mocked, scourged, beaten, and publicly crucified. Speak to Jesus, the Son of Man, about the price He paid to free you and what that means to you.

17

Made Right with God

To account something as true is not a matter of wishing or pretending. Accounting pertains to carefully balanced books. It is seeing a situation as it actually is. A person is accounted debt free not just based on hope or positive thinking but when confirmed by facts: no outstanding student loans, no mortgage or car payments, and so on. God declares you sin-free for the sake of Christ. He accounts you righteous and blameless, and you can bank on that!

GOD, YOU WANT ME TO KNOW THAT . . .

YOU HAVE JUSTIFIED ME

[God] poured out [the Holy Spirit] on us richly through Jesus Christ our Savior, so that *being justified by His grace* we might become heirs according to the hope of eternal life. (TITUS 3:6–7)

Related verses: Isaiah 45:25; Romans 3:24, 26; 4:25; 5:1, 15–16, 18; 8:30, 33; 1 Corinthians 6:11; Galatians 2:16; 3:24.

Justification **is a legal term, indicating acquittal from guilt. Solely by the grace of your Savior, Jesus Christ, all charges against you have been dropped. With the Holy Spirit's help, admit to Jesus how His justifying is vastly superior to your own self-justification, and recognize with Him what His justification makes possible in your life.**

GOD, YOU WANT ME TO KNOW THAT . . .

YOU HAVE ACCOUNTED ME RIGHTEOUS

Out of the anguish of His soul [the Lord] shall see and be satisfied; *by His knowledge shall the Righteous One, My servant, make many to be accounted righteous*, and He shall bear their iniquities. (ISAIAH 53:11)

Related verses: Psalm 103:17; Jeremiah 23:6; Romans 3:20–22; 8:3–4; 2 Corinthians 5:21; James 2:23.

Envision your personal Righteousness Account Statement as a three-column spreadsheet, where the first column is labeled ***My Debt***, the second is ***What Christ Paid for Me***, and the last is ***Balance Due***. Give examples of some entries on that spreadsheet. What is the grand total in the ***Balance Due*** column? Respond from your heart to your Lord for bearing your iniquities and thereby canceling your debt.

18

Made Holy and Blameless

Fill in your name: St. ____________________? God invites you to trade in the filthy rags of your own self-righteousness for the radiant-white robe of Christ's righteousness. He declares you clean and calls you His saint, His "holy one." He has deliberately set you apart for His own special purposes. Thanks to Christ you are now in fact His saint!

GOD, YOU WANT ME TO KNOW THAT . . .

YOU HAVE MADE ME HOLY

[God] chose us in [the Lord Jesus Christ] before the foundation of the world, that we should be holy and blameless before Him. (EPHESIANS 1:4)

Related verses: Isaiah 62:12; Luke 1:74–75; Romans 1:7; 1 Corinthians 1:30; 6:11; Colossians 1:22; Hebrews 2:11; 10:10; 1 Peter 1:2.

Picture Jesus proudly presenting you to His Father as holy to Him. Describe the scene to God and thank Him that this is your reality.

GOD, YOU WANT ME TO KNOW THAT . . .

YOU HAVE WASHED ME CLEAN

But *you were washed*, you were sanctified, you were justified *in the name of the Lord Jesus Christ and by the Spirit of our God.* (1 CORINTHIANS 6:11)

Related verses: Ezekiel 36:25, 33; 37:23; Zechariah 13:1; John 15:3; Acts 15:9; Titus 3:5–6; Hebrews 10:22; 1 John 1:9.

Have you ever been embarrassed by having a smudge on your face or food stuck between your teeth at a formal gathering? Imagine the shame of standing before God, hideously filthy in your sins. Express to Jesus what it means to you that He Himself has thoroughly washed you.

GOD, YOU WANT ME TO KNOW THAT . . .

YOU HAVE PROVIDED ME THE ROBE OF RIGHTEOUSNESS

I will greatly rejoice in the Lord; my soul shall exult in my God, for He has clothed me with the garments of salvation; He has covered me with the robe of righteousness, as a bridegroom decks himself like a priest with a beautiful headdress, and as a bride adorns herself with her jewels. (ISAIAH 61:10)

Related verses: Psalm 149:4; Isaiah 1:18.

In Jesus' time, wedding guests were furnished standard robes so all could mingle equally. In the parable found in Matthew 22:11–14, a wedding guest refuses to wear the wedding garment freely provided to him upon entry and so is cast out. Consider with God what that implies for trying to

enter Christ's kingdom without wearing His freely provided robe of righteousness.

GOD, YOU WANT ME TO KNOW THAT . . .

YOU HAVE PURIFIED ME

[We are] waiting for our blessed hope, the appearing of the glory of *our great God and Savior Jesus Christ, who gave Himself for us* to redeem us from all lawlessness and *to purify for Himself a people for His own possession* who are zealous for good works. (TITUS 2:13–14)

Related verses: Malachi 3:3; Hebrews 9:14; 1 Peter 1:22–23; 1 John 3:2–3; Revelation 21:2, 9–11.

Tell Jesus what it means to you that He has graciously purified you—removing from you everything that would have disqualified you from being in His presence.

19

At Peace with God

When someone close to you is disappointed, upset, or angry with you, life can become stressful and unpleasant. Tensions may mount, and a dark cloud may hover over you. Are you sometimes keenly aware of your failures before God and how you have repeatedly disappointed Him? Such realizations might lead you to promise to try harder next time or to justify yourself and make excuses or just give up and try to hide from Him. You might even wonder if you have sinned against God one too many times, leaving you uncertain of His ongoing love and approval. The amazing truth is that, in love, Christ died in your place, paying in full for every one of those sins. In Christ, no condemnation or judgment remains. Be reassured that God loves you perfectly and enables nothing less than perfect peace for you in your relationship with Him. So long, dark cloud!

GOD, YOU WANT ME TO KNOW THAT . . .

YOU HAVE ESTABLISHED PERFECT PEACE FOR ME

Therefore, since we have been justified by faith, *we have peace with God through our Lord Jesus Christ.* (ROMANS 5:1)

Related verses: Isaiah 54:10; Luke 2:14; Ephesians 2:14–15, 17; Colossians 1:19–20.

What is the significance of being at peace with God? Trace with Him all that He has done to establish this peace.

GOD, YOU WANT ME TO KNOW THAT . . .

YOU HAVE RECONCILED ME TO YOURSELF

If while we were enemies we were reconciled to God by the death of His Son, much more, now that we are reconciled, shall we be saved by His life. More than that, we also rejoice in God through our Lord Jesus Christ, through whom we have now received reconciliation. (ROMANS 5:10–11)

Related verses: 2 Corinthians 5:18–19; Ephesians 2:13; Colossians 1:20–22.

God positioned the earth at just the right distance from the sun for life to thrive. Imagine what would happen if our planet started to drift away from the sun. The term *reconcile* literally means "to restore to a proper orbit or relationship." Communicate to God about the importance of you having been reconciled to Him.

HE ALSO GLORIFIED ME

ROMANS 8:30

You are a new creation; the old has passed away and the new has come. You are being transformed from darkness into brilliant light. Marvel at the following ways in which God in Christ has already glorified you.

20

Old Self Died

Your new life begins with your death! Your old, sinful nature, inherited from your original parents, Adam and Eve, cannot be reformed or rehabilitated. It must instead be put to death. It does no good to dress your old self in formal wear; it must be completely done away with. Self-help books are useful for various aspects of life, but when it comes to your sinful nature and being right with God, self-help can only make things worse. God has provided you the only viable solution. Since you by faith have participated in Christ's death, your slavery to sin has been ended, the claims of the Law on you have been set aside, and your heart of stone has been removed.

GOD, YOU WANT ME TO KNOW THAT . . .

I HAVE BEEN CRUCIFIED WITH CHRIST

***I have been crucified with Christ.* It is no longer I who live, but Christ who lives in me.** (GALATIANS 2:20)

We were buried therefore with [Christ Jesus] by baptism into death. (ROMANS 6:4)

Related verses: Romans 6:4–5, 8; 2 Corinthians 5:14; Philippians 3:10; Colossians 2:12; 3:3.

Through Baptism, you have died along with your Lord Jesus Christ. On the cross, He took your place and decisively broke the shackles of your old, sinful nature. Thank Him for the reality and implications of having been crucified with Him.

GOD, YOU WANT ME TO KNOW THAT . . .

I HAVE DIED TO SIN

[Christ] Himself bore our sins in His body on the tree, that we might die to sin and live to righteousness. (1 PETER 2:24)

Related verses: Romans 6:6–7, 11, 18, 22; 7:24–25; 2 Peter 1:4.

Trace with Jesus Christ what having died to sin means in your life and what this has made possible for you.

GOD, YOU WANT ME TO KNOW THAT . . .

I HAVE DIED TO THE LAW

Likewise, my brothers, *you also have died to the law through the body of Christ*, so that you may belong to another, to Him who has been raised from the dead, in order that we may bear fruit for God. (ROMANS 7:4)

Related verses: Romans 10:4; Galatians 2:19.

God's Law can only condemn you if you are alive to it. Consider with God the implications of the fact that you have died to the Law.

GOD, YOU WANT ME TO KNOW THAT . . .

YOU REMOVED MY HEART OF STONE

[The Lord God says,] "*I will take out your stony, stubborn heart* and give you a tender, responsive heart." (EZEKIEL 36:26 NLT)

Related verse: Ezekiel 11:19.

Some characteristics of having a "stony, stubborn heart" include being uncaring, resentful, arrogant, and unyielding to God. Recognize before your Lord why it was crucial that He removed your heart of stone.

21

New Self Created

Perhaps at times you may feel that little about you has actually changed. You look the same in the mirror, and you tend to give in to many of the same temptations. But God wants you to know for a fact that the changes He has worked in you are very real and are critical for your life today and into eternity. Since you have died with Christ, so also you have been made alive with Him. You are, in fact, a new creation—in the process of being conformed to Jesus. You have been reborn and have been given a new heart and spirit designed to align with God's own heart. You have been enabled to bear genuine fruit for Him. The old has indeed passed away, and all things have become new for you. Please know that God's Word is far more accurate and dependable than your feelings or perceptions could ever be!

GOD, YOU WANT ME TO KNOW THAT . . .

I'M YOUR NEW CREATION

Therefore, if anyone is in Christ, he is a new creation. The old has passed away; behold, the new has come. (2 CORINTHIANS 5:17)

Related verses: 1 Corinthians 15:49; Galatians 6:15; Ephesians 4:24; James 1:18.

The fact that God masterfully created you is, in itself, a great wonder. Contemplate with Jesus Christ what all might be included in God having made you a *new* creation.

GOD, YOU WANT ME TO KNOW THAT . . .

YOU HAVE GIVEN ME A NEW BIRTH

Blessed be the God and Father of our Lord Jesus Christ! According to His great mercy, He has caused us to be born again to a living hope through the resurrection of Jesus Christ from the dead. (1 PETER 1:3)

Related verses: John 1:13; 1 Peter 1:23; 1 John 3:9; 4:7; 5:1, 4, 19.

Recount to God the Father how you have been born again to a living hope and why that's vital to you.

GOD, YOU WANT ME TO KNOW THAT . . .

YOU HAVE GIVEN ME A NEW HEART

[The Lord God says,] "I will give you a new heart, and a new spirit I will put within you." (EZEKIEL 36:26)

The Lord your God will circumcise your heart and the heart of your offspring, so that you will love the Lord your God with all your heart and with all your soul, that you may live. (DEUTERONOMY 30:6)

Related verses: Psalm 37:31; Jeremiah 31:33; 32:40; Ezekiel 11:19; Ephesians 2:10; Hebrews 12:23.

Now that the Lord your God has completed His divine heart transplant in you, explore with Him all that has changed and is still changing in you.

22

Made Alive through Christ

One day I was driving around a business campus in a distant city, searching for the building where training was to take place. I finally just walked into one of the buildings and asked the receptionist for directions to my destination. She replied, "Sir, you are in it."

Do you ever find yourself searching for something that helps make your Christian experience more vibrant, more authentic, more meaningful, or more effective? If only you could figure out what was lacking, life might be so much better. Great news! In Christ, the new you has already been infused with true life, and you have been fully empowered to become and do all God has planned for you. You have been set free to serve God without fear. His Spirit lives in you and is with you every moment of every day. There is no need to search anymore, because in Christ, you are already right where you need to be.

GOD, YOU WANT ME TO KNOW THAT . . .

YOU HAVE MADE ME ALIVE TO YOU

So you also must consider yourselves dead to sin and alive to God in Christ Jesus. (ROMANS 6:11)

Related verses: Luke 20:38; Romans 5:18; 8:11; 1 Corinthians 15:22; Galatians 2:19–20; Ephesians 2:5; Colossians 2:12–13; 1 John 4:9; 5:12.

Recall with Jesus Christ some of the ways in which you have been made alive in Him.

GOD, YOU WANT ME TO KNOW THAT . . .

YOU HAVE MADE ME ALIVE TO RIGHTEOUSNESS

[Christ] Himself bore our sins in His body on the tree, that we might die to sin and live to righteousness. (1 PETER 2:24)

Related verses: Luke 1:74–75; Romans 5:21; 6:7–8, 18, 22; 8:10.

Without Christ, the righteousness required of you is both unattainable and condemning. Express to Jesus Christ what is now different in you regarding righteousness.

23

Received Grace upon Grace

But wait—there's more!" This phrase, found in countless commercials, might have introduced every topic in this book. You have come to know that you are perfectly loved and completely forgiven. God in Christ has accomplished everything for you, and all is now fully in place. He has given you new, unending life, and He is perfectly capable of building upon the foundation that He has established in you. He has also provided you with everything you will need to effectively live out the adventure He's prepared for you and to reflect His glorious light to those around you.

GOD, YOU WANT ME TO KNOW THAT . . .

YOU HAVE GLORIFIED ME

Those whom [God] predestined He also called, and those whom He called He also justified, and *those whom He justified He also glorified.* (ROMANS 8:30)

Related verses: Isaiah 9:2; 55:5; Ephesians 2:4–6; 5:8; 1 Peter 2:9.

In 1 Corinthians 15:41, Paul notes that the "glory" of the sun and moon differ. In fact, the moon produces no light of its own but instead is illuminated by the sun's glory. Similarly, whenever others view spiritual light from you, it is a reflection of God's glory. Determine with Him what is taking place when others are drawn into a deeper faith in Him through encountering you.

GOD, YOU WANT ME TO KNOW THAT . . .

YOU HAVE GIVEN ME EVERY GOOD THING

I pray that the sharing of your faith may become effective for the full knowledge of every good thing that is in us for the sake of Christ. (PHILEMON 6)

From [Jesus Christ's] fullness we have all received, grace upon grace. (JOHN 1:16)

Related verses: Psalm 84:11; Romans 8:32; 2 Corinthians 9:8; Hebrews 12:28.

I pray that God's "yesterday" promises and assurances have enhanced your understanding of all that is now yours in Christ—truly grace heaped upon grace! Declare to God several of His gracious promises that have especially encouraged and assured you. Celebrate these now!

Standing firmly upon the solid base of God's *yesterday* promises and assurances, you are now warmly invited to explore and savor the amazing world of God's *today* promises and assurances for you!

TODAY

That you may know . . . what is the immeasurable greatness of [God's] power toward us who believe.

EPHESIANS 1:18–19

In Dan Stone's book *The Rest of the Gospel*, coauthored with David Gregory, Dan compares his experience of life as a Christian to a bed—with the *yesterday* facts about Christ's sacrifice like a sturdy headboard and the *forever* promises of eternal life like a solid footboard. But God's *today* assurances in his daily life had seemed to him more like a sagging, lumpy mattress. Can you relate? The reality is that God is just as active, engaged, and purposeful in your life now as He was during Christ's resurrection and as He will be at Christ's glorious return. That exact same power is at work in you today!

Perhaps you are uneasy about God's striking promises and assurances for your life right now. Maybe you fear that they are too good to be true, or you judge yourself unworthy of them. Or possibly you are afraid to really bank on such promises. What if they don't come true, or what if your faith isn't strong enough? If it just depended on you, you would have genuine reason for concern. And not just you, but everyone who has ever walked this planet other than God and His Son.

God winsomely invites you into the incredible adventure of life in and with Him in the here and now. The following assurances were not written just for others; they are written for *you*. God wants you to treasure and experience all He has for you. Are you ready to trade in that old mattress?

I AM GOD'S BELOVED

Why does God provide you so many promises and assurances? I am convinced it is because God is both the source and essence of love, and He so much wants you to know and experience that love. Following is a special opportunity for you to delight in several aspects of His amazing love for you today.

24

God Loves Me Dearly

Let's start by recognizing some lies you may have been telling yourself. Perhaps you have felt like you are a marginal, insignificant Christian. Maybe you doubt you will ever amount to much or that God has any significant plans for your life. Well, guess again! The amazing truth is that you are greatly loved, intimately known, freely welcomed, and richly blessed by your Lord. Because of His love for you, you have so very much to look forward to!

GOD, YOU WANT ME TO KNOW THAT . . .

YOU LOVE ME GREATLY

But God, being rich in mercy, because of *the great love with which He loved us*, even when we were dead in our trespasses, made us alive together with Christ—by grace you have been saved. (EPHESIANS 2:4–5)

Related verses: Hosea 2:14; Zephaniah 3:17; John 16:27; Romans 1:7; 5:5; 8:39; 9:25; Ephesians 3:19; 2 Corinthians 13:11.

Let the almighty God, the Creator of the universe, know what it means to you that He greatly loves *you*.

GOD, YOU WANT ME TO KNOW THAT . . .

YOU KNOW ME THROUGH AND THROUGH

O Lord, You have searched me and known me! You know when I sit down and when I rise up; You discern my thoughts from afar. You search out my path and my lying down and are acquainted with all my ways. Even before a word is on my tongue, behold, O Lord, You know it altogether. (PSALM 139:1–4)

[Jesus said,] "Why, even the hairs of your head are all numbered." (LUKE 12:7)

Related verses: Psalm 1:6; 37:18; Isaiah 49:16; Jeremiah 12:3; John 10:14, 27; 1 Corinthians 8:3; Galatians 4:9; 2 Timothy 2:19.

✎ Consider with the Lord God how His thorough knowledge of you might seem intimidating at first, but how it is, in fact, a truly wonderful thing.

GOD, YOU WANT ME TO KNOW THAT . . .

YOU WELCOME ME FREELY

Therefore welcome one another as *Christ has welcomed you*, for the glory of God. (ROMANS 15:7)

Related verses: Psalm 56:9; 59:10; Ezekiel 20:41; Hosea 14:4; Acts 10:35; Ephesians 2:18; 3:12.

✎ Imagine how it might feel to be welcomed by a friend, your boss, a celebrity, or a world leader. Tell Jesus Christ how it feels to be wholeheartedly welcomed by Him.

GOD, YOU WANT ME TO KNOW THAT . . .

YOU BLESS ME RICHLY

You bless the righteous, O Lord. (PSALM 5:12)

Related verses: Numbers 6:24; Psalm 41:2; 67:6; 115:12–13; Isaiah 44:3; 61:9; Jeremiah 17:7; Ezekiel 34:26; Luke 11:28.

To be blessed by God means to be the focus of His delight and the recipient of His grace, gifts, and protection. Recount to the Lord some of the ways in which He has blessed you.

25

Immanuel—God Is with Me

How would you define *religion*? Some may see it as a system of beliefs and traditions, a philosophy of life and behavior, or an elevated state of mind. But when God promised the coming of Jesus, the Messiah, He introduced Him as *Immanuel*, which means "God with us." God is so much more than a concept or an ideal. God is not an *it* but rather a *He*. *He* has come to be with you, *He* sent His Son to die for you, and *He* desires to develop an intimate, vibrant relationship with you. You are always on His mind; He dearly desires to be on yours as well.

GOD, YOU WANT ME TO KNOW THAT . . .

YOU ARE WITH ME

Fear not, for *I am with you*; be not dismayed, for *I am your God*. (ISAIAH 41:10)

[Jesus said,] "Behold, I am with you always, to the end of the age." (MATTHEW 28:20)

Related verses: Deuteronomy 31:8; Psalm 23:4; Amos 5:14; Zephaniah 3:17; Matthew 1:23; John 14:23; 1 Corinthians 1:9; 2 Corinthians 13:4; Philippians 4:9.

Perhaps you have experienced intense loneliness due to a pandemic or other isolating situations. Reflect with God on the implications of His *always* being with you.

GOD, YOU WANT ME TO KNOW THAT . . .

YOU ARE MY GOD

O God, You are my God; earnestly I seek You; my soul thirsts for You. (PSALM 63:1)

[The Lord said,] "I will give them a heart to know that I am the LORD, and they shall be My people and I will be their God." (JEREMIAH 24:7)

Related verses: Genesis 17:7; Leviticus 11:45; 26:12; Deuteronomy 30:6; 1 Kings 8:23; 1 Chronicles 17:22; Isaiah 25:1; 41:13; Zechariah 13:9; Galatians 4:9; Hebrews 11:16.

God is pleased to be your God, and He has absolutely committed Himself to His relationship with you. Thank Him for giving you a heart that knows that He is your God.

GOD, YOU WANT ME TO KNOW THAT . . .

YOU ENABLE ME TO KNOW YOU

No longer shall each one teach his neighbor and each his brother, saying, "Know the LORD," for *they shall all know Me, from the least of them to the greatest*, declares the LORD. (JEREMIAH 31:34)

Related verses: Exodus 6:7; John 10:14; Galatians 4:9; Hebrews 8:11; 1 John 2:13–14.

✎ Trace how you have come to know God more completely over your lifetime so far. Ask your Lord to enable you to know Him more and more.

GOD, YOU WANT ME TO KNOW THAT . . .

I'M IN YOUR PRESENCE AND ON YOUR MIND

Then those who feared the Lord spoke with one another. The Lord paid attention and heard them, and a book of remembrance was written before Him of those who feared the Lord and esteemed His name. (MALACHI 3:16)

You have kept count of my tossings; put my tears in Your bottle. Are they not in Your book? (PSALM 56:8)

Related verses: Job 7:18; Psalm 40:5, 17; 73:23; Isaiah 66:14; Matthew 10:30; 1 Peter 3:12.

✎ Express your amazement to the Lord your God that there is nothing about you or the challenges that you face that gets less than His full focus and involvement.

26

Drawn Near

Much like gravity keeps you securely on earth, so sin exerts a powerful draw on you. On a low-humidity day, try placing a tiny scrap of tissue on a table. Run a comb through your hair and hold it just above the tissue. The tissue jumps to the comb above because the force of electricity from a couple of extra electrons completely overpowers the force of gravity from the entire earth below. In effect, the law of static electricity has set the tissue free from the law of gravity.

Paul uses similar language when he tells you that the law of the Spirit of life in Christ Jesus has set you free from the law of sin and death (Romans 8:2). God in Christ draws you to Himself, breaking sin's death grip on you. You have been brought near to God by Christ's blood, and now He comes to you, rejoices over you, and lives in you. Christ was lifted up on the cross for you, and now you are being drawn mightily to Him. Sin and death don't stand a chance!

GOD, YOU WANT ME TO KNOW THAT . . .

YOU DRAW ME TO YOURSELF

[Jesus said,] "No one can come to Me unless the Father who sent Me draws him." (JOHN 6:44)

[Jesus said,] "I, when I am lifted up from the earth, will draw all people to Myself." (JOHN 12:32)

Related verses: Jeremiah 31:3; Hosea 11:4; Ephesians 2:13; Hebrews 7:19, 25.

Explain how the fact that Jesus draws you to Himself is a delightful blessing. Share with Him how you have personally experienced His draw.

GOD, YOU WANT ME TO KNOW THAT . . .

YOU COME TO ME

[Jesus said,] "Behold, I stand at the door and knock. If anyone hears My voice and opens the door, *I will come in to him and eat with him, and he with Me.*" (REVELATION 3:20)

Related verses: Leviticus 26:11; Psalm 34:18; 2 Corinthians 6:16; James 4:8.

Consider with Jesus the importance of this fact: you do not come to Him, but He comes to you to fellowship with you.

GOD, YOU WANT ME TO KNOW THAT . . .

YOU ARE PLEASED WITH ME

The Lord takes pleasure in His people. (PSALM 149:4)

Related verses: Psalm 147:11; Zephaniah 3:17; Luke 2:14; Hebrews 11:16.

Since you continue to sin, explore with the Lord how it is possible for Him to be *pleased* with you.

27

Greatly Favored

You may know someone who was deeply hurt when a spouse or friend suddenly announced that he or she had lost interest in the relationship and wanted out. Maybe this has happened to you. But rest assured that your faithful God will *never* reject you or leave you. Day after day, His friendship, favor, goodness, and mercies to you are never-ending. No exceptions!

GOD, YOU WANT ME TO KNOW THAT . . .

I AM YOUR FRIEND

[Jesus said,] "No longer do I call you servants, for the servant does not know what his master is doing; but *I have called you friends, for all that I have heard from My Father I have made known to you.*" (JOHN 15:15)

Related verses: Psalm 25:14; James 2:23.

Compare how different your relationships with friends are versus your relationships with casual acquaintances. Talk with Jesus about what it means to you that He calls you His friend.

GOD, YOU WANT ME TO KNOW THAT . . .

YOU SHOW YOUR GOODNESS TO ME

Surely goodness and mercy shall follow me all the days of my life, and I shall dwell in the house of the Lord forever. (PSALM 23:6)

Related verses: Psalm 13:6; 31:19; 73:1; 84:11; 86:5; 100:5; Jeremiah 32:40–42; Lamentations 3:25.

Recall various meanings and implications of the word ***goodness***. Let the Lord, your Shepherd, know what it means to you that His goodness always remains in effect and persistently follows you.

GOD, YOU WANT ME TO KNOW THAT . . .

YOU EXTEND YOUR UNENDING MERCY TO ME

The steadfast love of the Lord never ceases; *His mercies never come to an end; they are new every morning.* (LAMENTATIONS 3:22–23)

Related verses: Psalm 23:6; 103:4; 145:9; Luke 1:50; Ephesians 2:4; Hebrews 4:16.

When was the last day that you ***didn't*** need the Lord's mercy? Acknowledge to Him why it is a very good thing that His mercies to you are ***new every day***.

GOD, YOU WANT ME TO KNOW THAT . . .

YOU MAINTAIN YOUR FAITHFULNESS TO ME

All the paths of the LORD are steadfast love and faithfulness. (PSALM 25:10)

Great is Your faithfulness. (LAMENTATIONS 3:23)

Related verses: Exodus 34:6; Jeremiah 31:3; Micah 7:20; 1 Corinthians 10:13; 2 Thessalonians 3:3–5; 2 Timothy 2:13.

Name some individuals who have proven faithful to you. Recognize before the Lord how much more amazing is *His* faithfulness to you, and thank Him for this.

28

Fully Assured

How can you be sure that God's promises and assurances really apply to you today? My younger daughter once offered to provide party favors for a wedding reception. Wisely, the bride later called to check on her progress. Those who know my daughter, however, found this a little humorous, as she is very dependable and consistently completes projects on time with high quality.

So how well do you know God? What are your expectations of Him? Do you worry whether He is doing the absolute best for you? Do you fear that you had better look out for your own interests just in case He lets you down? Knowing Him and His character, there is absolutely no question that He will keep every last one of His promises to you.

How capable is God? He is almighty, great, and powerful.

How consistent is He? He is true, everlasting, and eternal.

How trustworthy is He? He is dependable, faithful, and steadfast.

How good is He? He is holy, righteous, perfect, and just.

How loving is He? He is caring, forgiving, patient, and kind.

How close is He? He is comforting, compassionate, and in you.

Any questions?

GOD, YOU WANT ME TO KNOW THAT . . .

YOU GIVE ME SURE PROMISES

His divine power has granted to us all things that pertain to life and godliness, through the knowledge of Him who called us to His own glory and excellence, *by which He has granted to us His precious and very great promises.* (2 PETER 1:3–4)

Related verses: Deuteronomy 4:31; Luke 1:72; 2 Corinthians 1:19–20; Galatians 4:28; Titus 1:2; Hebrews 6:17–19; 10:36.

God certainly makes you excellent promises and assurances. Add to these the amazing fact that God ***never*** lies (Numbers 23:19; Titus 1:2; Hebrews 6:18). Contemplate before God what this means for you.

GOD, YOU WANT ME TO KNOW THAT . . .

I HAVE CONFIDENCE BEFORE YOU

By this we shall know that we are of the truth and reassure our heart before Him; for whenever our heart condemns us, God is greater than our heart, and He knows everything. Beloved, if our heart does not condemn us, we have confidence before God. (1 JOHN 3:19–21)

In Christ Jesus our Lord . . . we have boldness and access with confidence through our faith in Him. (EPHESIANS 3:11–12)

Related verses: Psalm 27:1; Proverbs 3:26; Romans 5:5; 15:13; Hebrews 10:22; 1 Peter 5:10.

How could any imperfect person be confident before the holy and perfect God? Identify to Him your source of confidence from these verses, and declare to Him the confidence you are privileged to have.

GOD, YOU WANT ME TO KNOW THAT . . .

YOU WILL NEVER ABANDON ME

The Lord will not forsake His people; He will not abandon His heritage. (PSALM 94:14)

Related verses: Genesis 28:15; Deuteronomy 31:6; Psalm 9:10; 37:33; John 6:37; 2 Thessalonians 3:5.

A friend asks you, "What if I continue to disappoint God, and He gives up on me?" Describe to the Lord how you might encourage such a friend.

29

Deeply Comforted

During a loud thunderstorm in an unfamiliar place, a young child can become quite anxious and fearful. But in the reassuring arms of a parent, that same child can settle down, become peaceful, and even fall asleep. When Jesus found Himself weary and expended, He would head out to a remote place and spend time alone with His Father. God extends that same privilege to you. He knows how to set your heart at rest and to replace your fear and anxiety with His peace.

GOD, YOU WANT ME TO KNOW THAT . . .

YOU CARE FOR ME

Humble yourselves, therefore, under the mighty hand of God so that at the proper time He may exalt you, casting all your anxieties on Him, because *He cares for you.* (1 PETER 5:6–7)

Related verses: Exodus 22:27; Deuteronomy 32:10; Isaiah 41:10; Zechariah 10:3.

Meditate on the wholly unexpected fact that the God who created the universe genuinely cares about you individually. Share your thoughts with Him.

GOD, YOU WANT ME TO KNOW THAT . . .

YOU COMFORT ME

When the cares of my heart are many, Your consolations cheer my soul. (PSALM 94:19)

Blessed be the God and Father of our Lord Jesus Christ, the Father of mercies and God of all comfort, who comforts us in all our affliction, so that we may be able to comfort those who are in any affliction, with the comfort with which we ourselves are comforted by God. (2 CORINTHIANS 1:3–4)

Related verses: Psalm 116:8; Isaiah 66:13; Zephaniah 3:17; Matthew 11:29; 2 Thessalonians 2:16–17.

Reflect with the Lord about how He has often consoled and comforted you in the past and on the fact that He promises to continue to do this throughout your life.

GOD, YOU WANT ME TO KNOW THAT . . .

YOU ENABLE ME TO BE AT PEACE

Now may the Lord of peace Himself give you peace at all times in every way. (2 THESSALONIANS 3:16)

But *the fruit of the Spirit is* love, joy, *peace*, patience, kindness, goodness, faithfulness, gentleness, self-control. (GALATIANS 5:22–23)

Related verses: Numbers 6:26; Psalm 85:8; Isaiah 26:3, 12; 54:13; John 14:27; 16:33; 20:21; Romans 14:17; 15:13; Galatians 1:3; Philippians 4:7, 9; Colossians 3:15; 1 John 4:18.

Consider with your Lord Jesus Christ what it means for you to be truly at peace, particularly "at all times in every way." Thank Him for His promise of peace to you.

HE REVEALS HIMSELF TO ME

My wife and I have been married for decades. As you might guess, during our years together, we have come to know each other pretty well, but it's remarkable that we continue to learn new things about each other and ourselves. How well do you know God? Not only can you praise God for all that you already have learned, but you can also be excited about all you will continue to learn. Know for sure that He is deeply invested, through His Word and His Spirit, in enabling you to know Him more and more.

30

In God's Light

On one road trip, my family stopped to take a ride-through cave tour. Deep inside, our guide warned us she was about to extinguish all lights for a short time. I had never experienced such absolute darkness! I wasn't at all sure that I could have ever safely found my way out of that cave without some light source. God compares life without faith in Him to walking in darkness. Through the light of God's Word, you have experienced and come to know Him who is light. Only through Christ are you able to plainly see the truth about the darkness of your sin and the brilliance of His grace and glory. You are truly a child of light.

GOD, YOU WANT ME TO KNOW THAT . . .

I AM WALKING IN YOUR LIGHT

Again Jesus spoke to them, saying, "I am the light of the world. Whoever follows Me will not walk in darkness, but will have the light of life." (JOHN 8:12)

At one time you were darkness, but now you are light in the Lord. (EPHESIANS 5:8)

Related verses: Psalm 27:1; 36:9; 118:27; John 12:46; 1 Thessalonians 5:5.

Discern what it means that most people on earth are walking in spiritual darkness. Praise your Lord Jesus for His marvelous light, and pray both that you might always walk in it and that many more might genuinely experience it.

GOD, YOU WANT ME TO KNOW THAT . . .

I KNOW YOUR ABIDING TRUTH

The elder to the elect lady and her children, whom I love in truth, and not only I, but also *all who know the truth, because of the truth that abides in us and will be with us forever.* (2 JOHN 1–2)

When the Spirit of truth comes, He will guide you into all the truth. (JOHN 16:13)

Related verses: John 8:32; 1 Corinthians 2:10; 1 Timothy 2:4; 1 John 2:21.

In the first passage above, the aging apostle John was likely writing to the beloved members of a church, among whom the certain truth of God's Word was deeply believed and freely shared. Thank God for revealing His enduring truth to you through the ongoing guidance of His Holy Spirit and through your active participation in a congregation firmly anchored in God's Word.

31

God's Effective Word

You can learn a lot about God by considering the majesty and complexity of creation. You can also understand quite a bit about His Law, since that Law is written on your own heart. But there is only one place where you can accurately learn about His love and grace for you and about His plan for your life: His amazing love letter, the Bible. It is a book not about perfect people but about ordinary people like you in the hands of an extraordinary God. The Bible was inspired and written by God's Holy Spirit, and the Spirit is the one who enables you to understand it, believe it, and incorporate it into your life. As you read and meditate on God's Word, you become a dynamic part of His story. God's Word is truly alive and active in you!

GOD, YOU WANT ME TO KNOW THAT . . .

YOUR WORD IS NEAR ME

But *the word is very near you. It is in your mouth and in your heart*, so that you can do it. (DEUTERONOMY 30:14)

Related verses: Deuteronomy 6:5–7; Psalm 18:28; 119:103, 105; Isaiah 51:16.

Assess how intimately you are connected to the Word of God. Recount to the Lord your God how His Word creates hope and joy in you, even as it directs and empowers your life each day.

GOD, YOU WANT ME TO KNOW THAT . . .

YOUR WORD IS AT WORK IN ME

And we also thank God constantly for this, that when you received the word of God, which you heard from us, you accepted it not as the word of men but as what it really is, *the word of God*, which *is at work in you believers.* (1 THESSALONIANS 2:13)

Related verses: Psalm 19:8; 119:11, 24; Matthew 4:4; Luke 8:15; 1 Thessalonians 1:6; Hebrews 4:12; 1 John 2:14.

The Bible, God's Word, is how God makes Himself known to you, declares His will to you, and accomplishes His purposes in you. Invite Him to do His work in you through His Word. His answer will most assuredly be "Yes!" Share with Him how you have experienced His Word at work in you and others.

GOD, YOU WANT ME TO KNOW THAT . . .

I FIND YOUR SON IN YOUR WORD

[Jesus said,] "And the Father who sent Me has Himself borne witness about Me. . . . You search the Scriptures because you think that in them you have eternal life; and *it is they that bear witness about Me.*" (JOHN 5:37, 39)

Related verses: John 8:31–32; 2 Timothy 1:10; 3:15.

No one can properly read and apply the Bible without this one central truth: it all points to Jesus Christ. Recall before Jesus some of your favorite Bible accounts about Him.

32

God Is My Teacher

Some professions emphasize the importance of establishing a personal board of directors—a group of wise and experienced people who can help you avoid pitfalls and make informed decisions. How much greater value comes from consulting your wise and all-knowing God! You can think of the Father, Son, and Holy Spirit as your personal mentoring team, guiding you through the Scriptures and life. The Father gives you abundant wisdom and insight. Jesus makes the Father and Himself known to you and establishes in you His very own mind. The Holy Spirit enables you to receive all God has for you and to never forget Him.

GOD, YOU WANT ME TO KNOW THAT . . .

YOU TEACH ME

[The Lord declares,] "*All your children shall be taught by the* LORD, and great shall be the peace of your children." (ISAIAH 54:13)

Related verses: Psalm 25:14; 40:6; 94:12; Isaiah 28:26; 33:6; Matthew 7:7–8; 13:11; James 1:5.

GOD, YOU WANT ME TO KNOW THAT . . .

YOUR SON TEACHES ME

We know that *the Son of God has come and has given us understanding*, so that we may know Him who is true; and we are in Him who is true, in His Son Jesus Christ. He is the true God and eternal life. (1 JOHN 5:20)

Related verses: Luke 10:22; John 14:21; 15:15; 1 Corinthians 1:24; 2:16; Ephesians 3:18–19.

GOD, YOU WANT ME TO KNOW THAT . . .

YOUR SPIRIT TEACHES ME

[Jesus said,] "But the Helper, the Holy Spirit, whom the Father will send in My name, *He will teach you all things and bring to your remembrance all that I have said to you.*" (JOHN 14:26)

Related verses: John 16:13–15; 1 Corinthians 2:12; 1 John 2:20, 27.

We owe so much to our human teachers throughout the years, many of whom taught us on behalf of God Himself. Based on these verses, list for God several blessings you receive from Him—Father, Son, and Holy Spirit—as your Teacher. Consult with your Personal Mentoring Team regarding any questions you might have.

33

Talking with God

Have you seen this classic sitcom routine? Two people are discussing something about a third person who is standing nearby, as if he or she weren't there. That person may interject with irritation, "You know, I'm right here, and I can hear you." How often God must feel that way when we talk about Him as if He weren't really present and listening! What allows your faith to be more than a set of doctrines and principles, or a mere history lesson, is your interaction with the God to whom your faith points. You hear what He has to tell you. You talk to Him in prayer and in expectation, as a young child might with a parent. And God wants you to talk not only *about* Him but also *with* Him. Perhaps God is saying right now, "You know, I'm right here, and I can hear you."

GOD, YOU WANT ME TO KNOW THAT . . .

I KNOW YOUR SON'S VOICE

[Jesus said,] "*My sheep hear My voice*, and I know them, and they follow Me." (JOHN 10:27)

Jesus then said . . . , "If you continue in My word, you are truly My disciples." (JOHN 8:31 RSV)

Related verses: Isaiah 30:20–21; Jeremiah 31:34; John 10:14; Revelation 3:20.

Consider how you recognize and hear Jesus' voice, and tell Him why this is critical to you.

GOD, YOU WANT ME TO KNOW THAT . . .

YOU HEAR ME WHEN I CALL

[The Lord says,] "Then you will call upon Me and come and pray to Me, and I will hear you." (JEREMIAH 29:12)

[The Lord says,] "Before they call I will answer; while they are yet speaking I will hear." (ISAIAH 65:24)

Related verses: 2 Chronicles 7:14; Psalm 34:15; 145:18–19; Isaiah 58:9; Malachi 3:16; 1 John 5:14.

Acknowledge to the Lord what it means to you that He is constantly listening to you and that He hears your every prayer.

GOD, YOU WANT ME TO KNOW THAT . . .

YOU ANSWER MY PRAYERS

This is the confidence that we have toward [God], that if we ask anything according to His will He hears us. And if we know that He hears us in whatever we ask, we know that we have the requests that we have asked of Him. (1 JOHN 5:14–15)

Related verses: Psalm 91:15; Isaiah 65:24; Matthew 7:7–8, 11; 21:22; John 15:16; James 5:16.

This mind-boggling promise of answered prayer might fall outside your comfort zone. Yet God repeatedly encourages you to pray, and He assures you that your prayers in fact have "great power" (James 5:16). Describe to God what His promise of answered prayer means to you and present to Him any questions you might have about this.

Ask Him to help you more consistently discern His will for every situation.

GOD, YOU WANT ME TO KNOW THAT . . .

YOUR SPIRIT HELPS ME PRAY

Likewise the Spirit helps us in our weakness. For we do not know what to pray for as we ought, but the Spirit Himself intercedes for us with groanings too deep for words. And He who searches hearts knows what is the mind of the Spirit, because the Spirit intercedes for the saints according to the will of God. (ROMANS 8:26–27)

Related verse: Ephesians 6:18.

In our weakness, sometimes we find it challenging to admit or even think about the brokenness within ourselves or around us, much less talk with God about such matters. And when we do pray, we are often uncertain about what words to say. Thank the Holy Spirit for praying on your behalf to God and for focusing and enhancing any words that you speak.

34

Receiving His Counsel

Let's skip the clichéd jokes about men never asking for directions and admit that in our faith lives, we all too often go it alone. More troubling than not asking for directions is failing to know where you are going in the first place. God offers you full concierge services. He gives you His Word, renews your mind, and continually guides and advises you in your daily choices and decisions. In His unfailing love, He leads you in righteousness throughout your life's journey. He shepherds you and ensures that you are fed spiritually. He also directs you to walk according to His will for your life. You've got the smartest person in the world living inside you—*the* Counselor (John 14:26). Do you suppose it might be worth consulting with Him?

GOD, YOU WANT ME TO KNOW THAT . . .

YOU GUIDE ME

This is God, our God forever and ever. *He will guide us forever.* (PSALM 48:14)

I bless the Lord who gives me counsel; in the night also my heart instructs me. (PSALM 16:7)

Related verses: Exodus 15:13; Psalm 31:3; 73:24; Isaiah 58:11; Luke 1:79; John 14:16.

The Lord your God walks alongside you, always present to guide and counsel you. Through His Word, He transforms your mind and heart, enabling you to make wise choices and decisions. Recall to your guide specific times He has guided you.

GOD, YOU WANT ME TO KNOW THAT . . .

YOU LEAD ME

[The Lord says,] "I led them with cords of kindness, with the bands of love." (HOSEA 11:4)

You have led in Your steadfast love the people whom You have redeemed. (EXODUS 15:13)

Related verses: Deuteronomy 33:3; Psalm 23:2–3; 25:9; 31:3; 139:9–10; Galatians 5:18.

Your Lord stands before you, inviting you to follow Him. He wants you to fully participate in the purposeful adventure He has planned for you as His beloved child. Review for your leader some of the blessings you have experienced through learning to follow Him.

GOD, YOU WANT ME TO KNOW THAT . . .

YOU OVERSEE ME

[We] were straying like sheep, but have now returned to the Shepherd and Overseer of [our] souls. (1 PETER 2:25)

Related verses: Psalm 23:1; 80:1; 100:3; Jeremiah 3:15; Matthew 2:6.

Your Lord stands above you, faithfully serving as your Overseer. He enables you to confess your sins and orchestrates your growth as His child, even as He works all things together for your good. Share with your Overseer what makes it both safe and wise to fully submit to Him.

GOD, YOU WANT ME TO KNOW THAT . . .

YOU DIRECT MY PATH

May the Lord direct your hearts to the love of God and to the steadfastness of Christ. (2 THESSALONIANS 3:5)

You have made known to me the paths of life; You will make me full of gladness with Your presence. (ACTS 2:28)

Related verses: Deuteronomy 33:3; 2 Samuel 22:33; 1 Chronicles 29:18; Psalm 16:11; 25:12; Isaiah 26:7; Ezekiel 36:27.

Your Lord stands behind you, directing your path of life. Sometimes He chooses paths that you would not have chosen, but His direction is always in your best interest and tailored to accomplish His gracious purposes in the world. Thank your director for establishing your path of life. Bring to Him any questions or concerns that you may have. Ask Him to increase your faith in trusting His direction.

HE COMES TO MY AID

Who was your favorite superhero growing up? Mine was Superman, but you may have gravitated toward another. The mighty and good hero stands up against overwhelming odds to protect ordinary citizens from danger and evil. In that sense, superheroes are types of Christ. Christ prevailed at great cost in the epic battle between God's kingdom of light and the devil's realm of darkness. In Christ, you are never alone. The Lord is actively involved in your life and committed to protecting you. You can rest assured that He's got your back—and every other part of you, for that matter!

35

My Shepherd

If you were asked to design a mentoring program for a future king, what might it include? How about a multiyear assignment caring for helpless sheep in a little suburb of Jerusalem? No, that wouldn't have crossed my mind either, but it is the exact training that God provided for David, His future king! David's early years of protecting and caring for sheep taught him how later to care for his subjects. His beautiful and beloved Psalm 23 reflects how God is your Shepherd and how, as a result, you have everything you need. Your Shepherd tends to your needs, protects you from danger and predators, and guards you with His life. You learn to trust your Shepherd, even in scary times, and He comforts you and eases your fears. It's good to be one of His sheep!

GOD, YOU WANT ME TO KNOW THAT . . .

YOU KEEP ME

[The Lord] will not let your foot be moved; He who keeps you will not slumber. Behold, He who keeps Israel will neither slumber nor sleep. The Lord is your keeper; the Lord is your shade on your right hand. The sun shall not strike you by day, nor the moon by night. The Lord will keep you from all evil; He will keep your life. The Lord will keep your going out and your coming in from this time forth and forevermore. (PSALM 121:3–8)

Related verses: Psalm 12:7; 33:18; Proverbs 2:8; Isaiah 27:3; 40:11; 42:6; Hosea 11:4.

Here you are reminded that the Lord keeps you in so very many ways—He tirelessly and attentively watches over you, stabilizes you, limits threats and evil, preserves your life,

and facilitates your daily activities, both now and always. Acknowledge before your Good Shepherd these and other ways in which He has affectionately kept you.

GOD, YOU WANT ME TO KNOW THAT . . .

YOU CARRY ME

[The Lord says,] "Listen to Me, O house of Jacob, all the remnant of the house of Israel, who have been borne by Me from before your birth, carried from the womb; even to your old age I am He, and to gray hairs I will carry you. I have made, and I will bear; I will carry and will save." (ISAIAH 46:3–4)

[The Lord God] will tend His flock like a shepherd; *He will gather the lambs in His arms; He will carry them in His bosom*, and gently lead those that are with young. (ISAIAH 40:11)

Related verses: Deuteronomy 33:27; Psalm 68:19; Isaiah 63:9; John 10:28–29.

Have you seen an artist's rendition of Jesus tenderly carrying a sheep? Remember with your Good Shepherd some situations in which He has carried you and what these mean to you.

GOD, YOU WANT ME TO KNOW THAT . . .

YOU PROTECT ME

[The Lord says,] "Because he holds fast to Me in love, I will deliver him; *I will protect him*, because he knows My name." (PSALM 91:14)

We know that everyone who has been born of God does not keep on sinning, but *He who was born of God protects him*, and the evil one does not touch him. (1 JOHN 5:18)

Related verses: Psalm 4:8; 23:4; 41:2; 73:23; 91:11; 138:7; Proverbs 3:26; Zephaniah 3:15; Romans 16:20.

Sheep have many natural predators, and a good shepherd protects his sheep from them all. Identify to your Shepherd some of the dangers from which He has protected you.

36

My Savior

When facing grave danger from foes, you need a savior. When ancient Israel turned to God, He would raise up judges or saviors to rout their enemies and restore peace. What an incredible Savior you now have in your Lord Jesus Christ! He saves you from the power of evil and from God's wrath over sin. The Lord is indeed mighty to save you!

GOD, YOU WANT ME TO KNOW THAT . . .

YOU SAVE ME

Consequently, [*Jesus*] *is able to save to the uttermost those who draw near to God through Him*, since He always lives to make intercession for them. (HEBREWS 7:25)

Related verses: Psalm 37:40; 62:1, 6; 91:15; Isaiah 43:11; 46:4; 63:9; Habakkuk 3:18; 1 Peter 1:9.

Each day, a battle is being fought for your soul between God and His angels and the devil and his forces. Tell your Savior what it means to you that He actively saves you.

GOD, YOU WANT ME TO KNOW THAT . . .

YOU HELP ME

***My help comes from the Lord*, who made heaven and earth.** (PSALM 121:2)

Related verses: Psalm 38:22; 40:17; 54:4; 63:7; 124:8; Isaiah 41:10; Hebrews 1:14; 2:16; 4:16.

✎ Though we may fool ourselves, none of us is self-sufficient. What kinds of help do you need from the Lord? Bring these to Him right now in prayer, confident that He wants to help you.

GOD, YOU WANT ME TO KNOW THAT . . .

YOU WORK ON MY BEHALF

Oh, how abundant is Your goodness, which You have stored up for those who fear You and worked for those who take refuge in You, in the sight of the children of mankind! (PSALM 31:19)

Christ has entered, not into holy places made with hands, which are copies of the true things, but *into heaven itself, now to appear in the presence of God on our behalf.* (HEBREWS 9:24)

Related verses: Lamentations 3:58; Romans 8:34.

✎ We speak of people doing "the Lord's work," which is certainly appropriate (see 1 Corinthians 15:58). But how does it strike you to realize that God is also diligently working for you? Review the quoted and related verses above and recognize before your Lord how He is working on your behalf.

37

My Deliverer

So much is broken in our fallen world. We can fall prey to sorrow, disappointments, losses, broken appliances, accidents, injuries, illnesses, cancers, or damage from fire, water, wind, or hail. But none of these can ever cause a rift between you and your God. He knows exactly how to deliver and rescue you. He knows which trials will make you stronger and which must be resolved, as well as which struggles will make you a greater blessing to others and which would not. In all this, He wants you to know that He delights in rescuing you and works all for your good.

GOD, YOU WANT ME TO KNOW THAT . . .

YOU RESCUE ME

The Lord knows how to rescue the godly from trials. (2 PETER 2:9)

Related verses: 2 Samuel 22:20; Psalm 34:7; 37:40; 40:17; 50:15; 103:4.

Recall predicaments out of which God lovingly snatched you. Share with Him your amazement about how important He considers you.

GOD, YOU WANT ME TO KNOW THAT . . .

YOU MAKE ME MORE THAN A CONQUEROR

Who shall separate us from the love of Christ? Shall tribulation, or distress, or persecution, or famine, or nakedness, or danger, or sword? As it is written, "For Your sake we are being killed all the day long; we are regarded as sheep to be slaughtered." No, in all these things *we are more than conquerors through Him who loved us.* (ROMANS 8:35–37)

Related verses: Psalm 32:7; Hebrews 4:16.

A conqueror is one who is victorious over an enemy. Consider what it might mean that through your Lord Jesus Christ, you are *more* than a conqueror. Rejoice and give thanks to Him for this!

38

My Place of Refuge

An open field with hordes of enemies rapidly approaching is likely one of the last places you would choose to be left on your own. You would probably search desperately for a place of protection to hide yourself. Spiritually, you find yourself on such a battlefield. But the great news is that you have found a secure fortress in your Lord. Your life is built on the Rock that cannot be moved. In the day of distress, you can remain steadfast, for your life is safely and securely hidden in Christ.

GOD, YOU WANT ME TO KNOW THAT . . .

YOU ARE MY ROCK

The LORD lives, and blessed be my rock, and exalted be my God, the rock of my salvation. (2 SAMUEL 22:47)

Related verses: 2 Samuel 22:2, 32; 23:3; Psalm 18:46; 28:1; 61:2; 62:7; 78:35; 92:15; Isaiah 26:4; Matthew 7:24–25.

In the midst of the chaos and uncertainties of life, consider with God how He has proven to be your secure and immovable Rock.

GOD, YOU WANT ME TO KNOW THAT . . .

YOU ARE MY FORTRESS

O my Strength, I will sing praises to You, for *You, O God, are my fortress,* the God who shows me steadfast love. (PSALM 59:17)

Related verses: 2 Samuel 22:31, 33; Psalm 2:12; 28:8; 37:39; 46:7; 61:3; 62:2; 71:3; 91:2; Isaiah 25:4; 17:10.

A fortress is your stronghold, castle, or anything upon which you rely. Brainstorm before God several ways in which He is your fortress.

GOD, YOU WANT ME TO KNOW THAT . . .

YOU ARE MY HIDING PLACE

You are a hiding place for me; You preserve me from trouble; You surround me with shouts of deliverance. *Selah* (PSALM 32:7)

Related verses: Psalm 27:5; 91:1; 121:5–6.

The term ***Selah*** in a psalm probably cues a musical interlude, providing time for the hearer to pay special attention to what has just been stated. A ***hiding place*** is a private, secret place with God—an undisturbed, undistracted refuge with Him. Take a "Selah moment" and recall for the Lord your God some instances in which He has been your hiding place.

GOD, YOU WANT ME TO KNOW THAT . . .

YOU SPREAD YOUR WINGS OVER ME

He will cover you with His pinions, and under His wings you will find refuge. (PSALM 91:4)

Related verses: Deuteronomy 32:11; Psalm 36:7; 61:4.

Most of God's imagery of His relationship with you is male (father, husband, king), but here He compares Himself to a mother bird, sheltering her fledglings from predators and the elements. Explore with the Most High what it means to you to take refuge under the shelter of His wings.

39

My Strength and Shield

I remember a movie scene in which a man attempts to demonstrate his strength to a woman by shoving a large sofa through a small doorway. When she tells him that he can start pushing, he meekly replies, "I already did." Do you sometimes feel weak and inadequate as you attempt to do what God asks of you? If so, you are being quite realistic. Although you are weak, the Lord reminds you that *He* is your strength and your shield and that *His* strength is made perfect in your weakness.

GOD, YOU WANT ME TO KNOW THAT . . .

YOU ARE MY STRENGTH

God is our refuge and strength, a very present help in trouble. (PSALM 46:1)

Related verses: Psalm 18:1–2; 59:17; 89:17; Isaiah 41:10; Ephesians 6:10; 1 John 2:14.

Admit to God some situations that expose your weaknesses, and recognize how significant it is to you that He promises to be your strength.

GOD, YOU WANT ME TO KNOW THAT . . .

YOU ARE MY SHIELD

The Lord is my strength and my shield; in Him my heart trusts, and I am helped. (PSALM 28:7)

Related verses: Deuteronomy 33:29; Psalm 3:3; 18:35; 33:20; 84:11; 89:18; 91:4; 119:114; Proverbs 30:5; Acts 2:25.

Describe the purpose and importance of a shield. List and thank the Lord for several ways in which He serves as your shield.

HE ENABLES ME TO STAND

Life in this world can be very challenging. God sometimes allows extremely difficult situations to occur that you never would have chosen. But God doesn't leave you to fend for yourself. He remains with you on each journey through "the valley of the shadow of death" (Psalm 23:4), and He miraculously works even apparent disasters together for your good (Romans 8:28). It won't be long until these trials are gone forever, and you can be certain that, by His grace and power, at the end, you will still be standing.

40

Rescued from My Enemies

Ancient Israel's enemies are familiar, such as the Philistines, the Edomites, or the Amorites. Yet the real enemy of God's people was never other humans but rather the devil and his influence. Today this is just as true as ever. You face ill will and problems from those who are in rebellion against God. This might take the form of full-on persecution or of a more subtle loss of position, reputation, prestige, or credibility. Yet in all this, God still knows how to rescue you from your enemies. He protects you on every front. Nothing can happen to you without His permission and without somehow benefiting you. Jesus wants you to love and pray for your enemies, since your heavenly Father takes "no pleasure in the death of the wicked" (Ezekiel 33:11) but desires that everyone be saved (1 Timothy 2:4).

GOD, YOU WANT ME TO KNOW THAT . . .

YOU REVEAL MY TRUE ENEMY TO ME

Be sober-minded; be watchful. *Your adversary the devil* prowls around like a roaring lion, seeking someone to devour. (1 PETER 5:8)

We do not wrestle against flesh and blood, but against the rulers, against the authorities, against the cosmic powers over this present darkness, against the spiritual forces of evil in the heavenly places. (EPHESIANS 6:12)

Related verses: Ezekiel 33:11; 1 Timothy 2:4.

✎ When people hurt you, you may experience anger toward them. Ask God to open your eyes to see that your true enemy is the devil, not people, and pray now for individuals who have hurt you or those you love.

GOD, YOU WANT ME TO KNOW THAT . . .

YOU DELIVER ME FROM EVIL

Lead us not into temptation, but *deliver us from evil.* (MATTHEW 6:13)

But the Lord is faithful. He will establish you and guard you against the evil one. (2 THESSALONIANS 3:3)

Related verses: Psalm 23:4; 37:19; 121:7; 1 John 2:13–14.

✎ Like Paul, you know from experience that "evil lies close at hand" (Romans 7:21). Reflect with your Lord the significance of the following fact: He promises to deliver you from evil.

GOD, YOU WANT ME TO KNOW THAT . . .

YOU FIGHT ON MY BEHALF

You shall not fear them, for it is the LORD your God who fights for you. (DEUTERONOMY 3:22)

Related verses: Deuteronomy 20:4; 2 Samuel 22:18; Psalm 25:3; 41:2; 55:22; Zephaniah 3:15; Romans 8:31; 1 John 4:4.

On your own, you could never resist the onslaughts of the devil, the wicked world, or your own sinful nature. Assess before the Lord your God how the balance of power has shifted in you now that God fights for you.

GOD, YOU WANT ME TO KNOW THAT . . .

YOU EQUIP ME WITH YOUR ARMOR

Put on the whole armor of God, that you may be able to stand against the schemes of the devil. . . . Therefore take up the whole armor of God, that you may be able to withstand in the evil day, and having done all, to stand firm. Stand therefore, having fastened on the belt of truth, and having put on the breastplate of righteousness, and, as shoes for your feet, having put on the readiness given by the gospel of peace. In all circumstances take up the shield of faith, with which you can extinguish all the flaming darts of the evil one; and take the helmet of salvation, and the sword of the Spirit, which is the word of God. (EPHESIANS 6:11, 13–17)

Related verses: Isaiah 52:7; 59:17; 2 Corinthians 6:7; Hebrews 4:12.

Reflect upon the pieces of spiritual armor described in this passage. Suggest how some of them serve to equip you. Share with God some specific examples of how His armor has proven effective in your life.

41

Sharing in Christ's Suffering

Don't be surprised! The nonbelieving world treated Jesus horribly, so as His follower, should you really expect better treatment? Jesus' disciples rejoiced to be counted worthy to suffer for His name. Jesus forewarns you that those who hate Him will hate you as well. People in rebellion against God want to avoid or silence any reminders of God's involvement and authority in their lives. As you strive to live your life faithful to Him and His ways, you become unsettling to them. When persecution takes place, the Holy Spirit gives you words and wisdom for each situation. Be assured that restoration is coming and all persecution is only temporary. Unrepented evil will ultimately be charged against those who carry it out against you.

GOD, YOU WANT ME TO KNOW THAT . . .

YOU FOREWARN ME OF PERSECUTION

Indeed, all who desire to live a godly life in Christ Jesus will be persecuted. (2 TIMOTHY 3:12)

Related verses: Matthew 5:11–12; Romans 8:17; Philippians 3:10; 1 Peter 5:8–9.

At first glance, this might not sound much like a promise or assurance. But imagine the bewilderment experienced by those falsely led to expect life here on earth to always be prosperous and happy, if only they could muster up enough faith. Envision before the Lord Jesus Christ how this warning could be a blessing to you and how you might better respond to persecution when it happens.

GOD, YOU WANT ME TO KNOW THAT . . .

YOUR SPIRIT GIVES ME WORDS

[Jesus said,] "When they bring you to trial and deliver you over, do not be anxious beforehand what you are to say, but say whatever is given you in that hour, for it is not you who speak, but the Holy Spirit." (MARK 13:11)

Related verses: Matthew 10:18–20; Luke 12:11; 21:14–15; 1 Peter 4:14.

When people are cruel, heartless, and intent on causing you harm, it can be so difficult to speak words that will accomplish God's purposes. Talk to the Holy Spirit about the encouragement you find in this promise.

GOD, YOU WANT ME TO KNOW THAT . . .

YOU PROMISE MY RESTORATION

After you have suffered a little while, the God of all grace, who has called you to His eternal glory in Christ, will Himself restore, confirm, strengthen, and establish you. (1 PETER 5:10)

Related verses: Jeremiah 23:4; Ezekiel 34:28; Romans 8:35, 38–39; Galatians 1:4; 2 Thessalonians 1:5; Hebrews 13:6.

Jesus suffered and died for you, and now, because you are His follower, the godless world hates you as it hated Him.

Given Jesus' mighty victory on the cross against evil, explore with "the God of all grace" what is promised to you here.

GOD, YOU WANT ME TO KNOW THAT . . .

YOU PROVIDE JUSTICE FOR ME

[Jesus said,] "Will not God give justice to His elect, who cry to Him day and night? Will He delay long over them? I tell you, He will give justice to them speedily." (LUKE 18:7–8)

Related verses: Ezekiel 34:16; Micah 7:9.

In Psalm 10, the psalmist bemoans his observation that the wicked flourish and prosper, enjoying a rich life at the expense of others. Contemplate with God the implications of this justice-related assurance for your life, whether fulfilled in time or in eternity.

42

The Lord Supports Me

My wife and I enjoy taking walks together, and the local shopping mall is handy on hot, cold, or rainy days. But between the finish on the mall floors, the soles of my wife's shoes, and the angle of her steps, her foot can suddenly catch and cause her to stumble. We discovered that if she always holds my hand, however, she won't fall. Do you realize that God always figuratively holds your hand as you walk through life as His child? He supports and stabilizes you, sometimes through other people. When it comes to temptations, He sympathizes with your weaknesses, limits them, and provides you the way of escape. You are indeed in very good hands.

GOD, YOU WANT ME TO KNOW THAT . . .

YOU HOLD ME UP

[The Lord's servant] will be upheld, for the Lord is able to make him stand. (ROMANS 14:4)

Related verses: Deuteronomy 33:3; Psalm 18:35; 54:4; 119:165; 147:6; Isaiah 41:10.

Recall a recent challenging time in your life, and envision your Lord Jesus Christ walking alongside you and supporting you. Express your thanks to Him for doing precisely that!

GOD, YOU WANT ME TO KNOW THAT . . .

YOU KEEP ME FROM FALLING

The Lord makes firm the steps of the one who delights in Him; though he may stumble, he will not fall, for the Lord upholds him with His hand. (PSALM 37:23–24 NIV)

Related verses: 2 Samuel 22:34; Psalm 94:18; 119:165; 121:3; Jude 24–25.

We've all experienced times when we start to lose our footing, perhaps walking on an uneven surface or down a steep incline. Each of us also experiences moral or spiritual stumbles. Proclaim to the Lord your wonder and praise for all the times He has rebalanced you after such a stumble and has forgiven your sins.

GOD, YOU WANT ME TO KNOW THAT . . .

YOU ENABLE ME TO RESIST TEMPTATION

No temptation has overtaken you that is not common to man. God is faithful, and He will not let you be tempted beyond your ability, but with the temptation He will also provide the way of escape, that you may be able to endure it. (1 CORINTHIANS 10:13)

Because [Jesus] Himself has suffered when tempted, He is able to help those who are being tempted. (HEBREWS 2:18)

Related verses: Ezekiel 37:23; Matthew 6:13; Hebrews 4:15; James 1:13.

Consider with Jesus why He is able to help you whenever you are tempted to sin. Thank Him for this.

43

God Nurtures Me

Some people think that God got the universe started but that now He just sits back and watches what happens, as if it were a reality TV show. The fact is that in Christ, God actively preserves, sustains, and renews you moment by moment. He surrounds and protects you on all sides and makes and keeps you effective in faith and life. He is actively with you each step along the way, until one day you share fully with Him in His victory.

GOD, YOU WANT ME TO KNOW THAT . . .

YOU ENCIRCLE ME

You hem me in, behind and before, and lay Your hand upon me. (PSALM 139:5)

[*The Lord*] *encircled him*, He cared for him, He kept him as the apple of His eye. (DEUTERONOMY 32:10)

Related verses: Deuteronomy 31:8; Isaiah 58:8.

Have you ever carefully arranged foam peanuts or bubble wrap to safely secure an odd-shaped, breakable item for shipping? Recognize before the Lord how thoroughly and meticulously He wraps you in His arms and cares for you.

GOD, YOU WANT ME TO KNOW THAT . . .

YOU PRESERVE ME

As for You, O Lord, You will not restrain Your mercy from me; *Your steadfast love and Your faithfulness will ever preserve me!* (PSALM 40:11)

My flesh and my heart may fail, but God is the strength of my heart and my portion forever. (PSALM 73:26)

Related verses: Psalm 31:23; 32:7; 55:22.

Like all people, your enthusiasm can wane, your commitment can falter, and your memory can dim. Praise the Lord for His never-fading commitment to preserve you as His child—throughout your earthly life and into eternity.

GOD, YOU WANT ME TO KNOW THAT . . .

YOU KEEP ME VITAL

They who wait for the Lord shall renew their strength; they shall mount up with wings like eagles; they shall run and not be weary; they shall walk and not faint. (ISAIAH 40:31)

Related verses: Isaiah 57:15; Zechariah 10:3.

The problems and struggles of life can sap your energy and perhaps leave you wondering, "What's the use?" Meditate deeply on these promises, and report to the Lord how He refreshes you.

GOD, YOU WANT ME TO KNOW THAT . . .

YOU GRANT ME STEADFAST FAITH

"I will make them strong in the LORD, and they shall walk in His name," declares the LORD. (ZECHARIAH 10:12)

[Jesus said,] "I have prayed for you that your faith may not fail." (LUKE 22:32)

Related verses: Psalm 37:31; 1 Peter 1:7–8; 1 John 5:4–5.

So many forces are conspiring to undermine your faith, including the efforts of the devil (Mark 4:15), "the cares of the world and the deceitfulness of riches" (Mark 4:19), and the desires of the flesh, the desires of the eyes, and the pride of life (1 John 2:16). Acknowledge to the Lord the active role that He—Father, Son, and Holy Spirit—plays in securing your faith in the midst of it all.

I AM BEING TRANSFORMED

Does your life as a Christian ever feel like you are stuck in a loop with little growth or change? God views your situation very differently. He is passionate about orchestrating your sanctification, and He is in the business of constantly transforming you from glory into glory. By the ongoing work of the Holy Spirit through God's Word, the amazing adventure that He has called you to continues to unfold. Welcome to "the upward call of God in Christ Jesus" (Philippians 3:14)!

44

My Continuing Sanctification

I've always enjoyed seeing the bumper stickers that say, "Please be patient—God isn't finished with me yet." God has a design that He is masterfully carrying out in your life. Through His Spirit, He lovingly exposes and deals with your pet sins. He disciplines you as a loving Father, helping you to grow and mature. He reminds you that He is God and you are not, humbling and reorienting you. He never runs ahead of you or lags behind. He is carrying out the perfect growing experience, and when it comes to you, He never settles for second best. God be praised that you are still under construction!

GOD, YOU WANT ME TO KNOW THAT . . .

YOU RENEW ME

So we do not lose heart. Though our outer self is wasting away, our inner self is being renewed day by day. (2 CORINTHIANS 4:16)

Related verses: Leviticus 20:8; Job 7:17–18; Romans 8:29; 1 Corinthians 3:6–7; 1 Thessalonians 5:23; 2 Thessalonians 1:11; Hebrews 12:2.

Contemplate what it means to you to recognize that God's renewing activity is in full swing every day of your life. Express your thanks to God for this marvelous reality.

GOD, YOU WANT ME TO KNOW THAT . . .

YOU DISCIPLINE ME AS YOUR BELOVED CHILD

Know then in your heart that, as a man disciplines his son, the Lord your God disciplines you. (DEUTERONOMY 8:5)

Related verses: Psalm 94:12; Proverbs 3:12; Jeremiah 30:11; Hebrews 12:6–7, 10–11; Revelation 3:19.

Undergoing discipline may not be something you look forward to. But list for the Lord your God some of the wonderful things that come out of being disciplined by Him.

GOD, YOU WANT ME TO KNOW THAT . . .

YOU ENABLE ME TO FEAR YOU

[The Lord says,] "I will make with them an everlasting covenant, that I will not turn away from doing good to them. And *I will put the fear of Me in their hearts, that they may not turn from Me.*" (JEREMIAH 32:40)

I will establish My covenant with you, and you shall know that I am the Lord, that you may remember and be confounded, and never open your mouth again because of your shame, when I atone for you for all that you have done, declares the Lord God. (EZEKIEL 16:62–63)

Related verses: Ezekiel 36:31–32; Romans 3:19.

Although the promises in these verses might appear negative at first glance, examine their context. God sent prophets to the Southern Kingdom of Judah to warn them of

impending exile to Babylon for their unfaithfulness to God. He promised that when His children returned from exile, He would put fear of Him and respect in their hearts so they would not turn away from Him again. He promised that they would humbly remember their former sins and recognize God's gracious atonement for them. Rethink before the Lord how these unexpected assurances are, in fact, gracious gifts to you.

45

My Ongoing Sin Addressed

Let's talk about that matter of ongoing sin. You know you are fully forgiven in Christ, yet sin is still clearly present in your life. In John's first letter, he tells you not only that no one who is born of God continues to sin (3:9) but also that if you claim to have no sin, you call God a liar (1:10). So which is it? Actually, *both* are true! *Continuing* in sin involves knowing but not caring that what you are doing offends God and refusing to repent or change. As a Christian, your slavery to sin has been broken. You no longer make a *practice* of deliberately sinning. At the same time, the tendency for you to still sin out of weakness remains throughout your earthly life. Your Lord directs you to confess such sins to Him and to others, resulting in your forgiveness and cleansing.

GOD, YOU WANT ME TO KNOW THAT . . .

YOU PREVENT ME FROM PRACTICING SIN

No one born of God makes a practice of sinning, for God's seed abides in him; and he cannot keep on sinning, because he has been born of God. (1 JOHN 3:9)

Related verses: Romans 6:14; 7:24–25; 8:12; 2 Timothy 1:7; 1 John 5:18.

Is God's Holy Spirit convicting you at this time of any ongoing sin in your life, which up until now you have refused to confess to God? That's because God loves you and desires that you be set free from its grip on your heart. Confess it now to Him and experience His complete forgiveness.

GOD, YOU WANT ME TO KNOW THAT . . .

YOU ENABLE ME TO CONFESS MY SINS OF WEAKNESS

I acknowledged my sin to You, and I did not cover my iniquity; I said, "I will confess my transgressions to the LORD," and You forgave the iniquity of my sin. (PSALM 32:5)

Related verses: 1 John 1:8–9; 2:1.

Denying or making excuses for your sins of weakness seriously hampers your growth, effectiveness, and witness as a Christian. Recount to the Lord why daily repentance and confession are important in your life.

GOD, YOU WANT ME TO KNOW THAT . . .

YOU FORGIVE ME

If we say we have no sin, we deceive ourselves, and the truth is not in us. If we confess our sins, [God] is faithful and just to forgive us our sins and to cleanse us from all unrighteousness. (1 JOHN 1:8–9)

Related verses: 2 Chronicles 7:14; Psalm 32:5; 86:5; Isaiah 55:7; Mark 11:25; Luke 11:4.

Focus with God on how you might incorporate and celebrate the reality and implications of His priceless gift of forgiveness in Christ today.

46

Part of God's Household

You are growing as a member of God's family, learning to love those whom God loves and to serve Jesus by serving them. God gives you special roles in each season of your life. Some of those roles may be familiar and similar to what you have done in the past, while other roles may be excitingly or uncomfortably new. In any event, they are always valuable, fulfilling, and tailor-made by God just for you. Christ is a masterful builder of His holy temple, and you are an integral and unique part of it.

GOD, YOU WANT ME TO KNOW THAT . . .

YOU MAKE US ONE IN YOUR SON

[Jesus prayed,] "Holy Father, keep them in Your name, which You have given Me, that they may be one, even as We are one." (JOHN 17:11)

There is neither Jew nor Greek, there is neither slave nor free, there is no male and female, for *you are all one in Christ Jesus.* (GALATIANS 3:28)

Related verses: John 17:20–23; 1 Corinthians 12:13, 18, 27; Ephesians 2:19; 1 John 5:1.

Jesus' church on earth can become splintered over nonessential matters, dividing those for whom He died. Read John 17:20–23 and identify before Jesus reasons why He prayed to His Father that we might be one.

GOD, YOU WANT ME TO KNOW THAT . . .

YOU ARE BUILDING US INTO A TEMPLE

So then you are no longer strangers and aliens, but you are fellow citizens with the saints and members of the household of God, built on the foundation of the apostles and prophets, Christ Jesus Himself being the cornerstone, in whom the whole structure, being joined together, grows into a holy temple in the Lord. In Him you also are being built together into a dwelling place for God by the Spirit. (EPHESIANS 2:19–22)

Related verses: 1 Corinthians 3:9, 17; 6:19–20; 12:18; 2 Corinthians 6:16; Hebrews 3:6; 1 Peter 2:5.

Acknowledge before God the miracle of how He purposefully arranges you with other believers into just what's needed in every time and place.

47

New Realities

In Christ, all things are new for you! Among these new things is a wonderful freedom to pursue what pleases God—no longer out of fear or compulsion but simply because Christ has made it both possible and enjoyable to do so. By God's grace, the righteousness that is yours through faith makes you fully alive. You experience true joy, a sustainable and transforming sense of peace and well-being far more wonderful than fleeting episodes of happiness. You are also being transformed from glory into glory, becoming more like Jesus, and you will ultimately shine forever in eternity with Him. Praise God for all the marvelous gifts with which He has blessed you!

GOD, YOU WANT ME TO KNOW THAT . . .

YOU ENABLE ME TO EXPERIENCE TRUE FREEDOM

[Jesus said,] "So if the Son sets you free, you will be free indeed." (JOHN 8:36)

Related verses: John 8:32; Romans 6:22; Galatians 5:1, 13; 1 Peter 2:16.

As a believer in the Son of God, share with Him several things you have been set free *from*. Next, consider what you have been set free *for*.

GOD, YOU WANT ME TO KNOW THAT . . .

YOU MAKE ME TRULY ALIVE

I have been crucified with Christ. It is no longer I who live, but *Christ who lives in me. And the life I now live in the flesh I live by faith in the Son of God*, who loved me and gave Himself for me. (GALATIANS 2:20)

Related verses: Romans 5:17; Galatians 3:11; 2 Timothy 1:10.

Summarize for your Lord Jesus Christ how your life has been changed by faith in Him.

GOD, YOU WANT ME TO KNOW THAT . . .

YOU FILL ME WITH JOY

[Jesus said,] "These things I have spoken to you, that My joy may be in you, and that your joy may be full." (JOHN 15:11)

Related verses: Psalm 3:3; 4:7; 33:21; Acts 2:28; Romans 14:17; 15:13; 1 Peter 1:8; Jude 24.

While happiness is temporary and depends on your current circumstances, joy is enduring. Tell Jesus about the joy that you have come to experience as God's child.

GOD, YOU WANT ME TO KNOW THAT . . .

YOU MAKE ME RADIANT

Those who look to [the Lord] are radiant, and their faces shall never be ashamed. (PSALM 34:5)

We all, with unveiled face, beholding the glory of the Lord, are being transformed into the same image from one degree of glory to another. For this comes from the Lord who is the Spirit. (2 CORINTHIANS 3:18)

Related verses: Psalm 3:3; 62:7; Isaiah 55:5; 2 Thessalonians 1:12.

An accomplished gem cutter knows how to create facets at just the right angles, such that the diamond-in-progress becomes progressively able to reflect the light that shines into it. Compare this to what the Lord is in the process of accomplishing in you, and express to Him your appreciation.

I EXPERIENCE NEW LIFE

How does your Christian life appear to you? Do you seem to be merely making do or scraping by? If so, you could definitely benefit from new lenses. God has blessed you with every spiritual blessing in Christ, and He has put everything in place for you to live abundantly and to be fully satisfied. He supplies all you could need and withholds nothing from you. May you see with enhanced clarity the new life that God so lovingly and lavishly provides for you.

48

Blessed Abundantly

A few years ago, my wife began a Thanksgiving tradition with our extended family. We take turns around the table, sharing blessings for which each of us is thankful to God. It is always so encouraging to recall and celebrate the goodness of the Lord among us. Here you are invited to marvel anew at God's rich and abundant blessings to you. May you truly feast upon these!

GOD, YOU WANT ME TO KNOW THAT . . .

YOU GIVE ME ABUNDANT LIFE

[Jesus said,] "I came that they may have life and have it abundantly." (JOHN 10:10)

Blessed be the God and Father of our Lord Jesus Christ, who has blessed us in Christ with every spiritual blessing in the heavenly places. (EPHESIANS 1:3)

Related verses: Psalm 30:5; 31:19; 36:8; Isaiah 58:11; Romans 6:4; 8:32; 2 Corinthians 3:6.

Based on the quoted and related verses above, list for Jesus what the abundant life that He promises includes.

GOD, YOU WANT ME TO KNOW THAT . . .

YOU SATISFY MY SOUL

[The Lord] satisfies the longing soul, and the hungry soul He fills with good things. (PSALM 107:9)

Related verses: Psalm 23:3; 63:5; 1 Peter 5:10.

Reflect on a time when your soul was longing or hungry. Thank the Lord for satisfying your soul and for filling it with good things.

49

Physical Needs Supplied

God knows you need food, clothes, shelter, and health to function in this world. After all, He made you the way you are, and Jesus personally experienced all these same needs as He lived among us. Jesus assures you that as you seek what is important to God, God commits Himself to meeting your physical needs as well (Matthew 6:33). He often satisfies these needs through your productive work, regular exercise, and healthy lifestyle, as all along you look to Him as your Provider and Great Physician.

GOD, YOU WANT ME TO KNOW THAT . . .

YOU MEET ALL MY NEEDS

My God will supply every need of yours according to His riches in glory in Christ Jesus. (PHILIPPIANS 4:19)

Related verses: Psalm 23:1; 34:9; 1 Timothy 6:17.

Contemplate before God why it might be that you don't always get what you think you need at the time when you think you need it.

GOD, YOU WANT ME TO KNOW THAT . . .

YOU CLOTHE ME

[Jesus said,] "Consider the lilies, how they grow: they neither toil nor spin, yet I tell you, even Solomon in all his glory was not arrayed like one of these. But if God so clothes the grass, which is alive in the field today, and tomorrow is thrown into the oven, how much more will He clothe you, O you of little faith!" (LUKE 12:27-28)

Related verses: Matthew 6:28–30; Luke 12:30–31.

Whether you worry about how you will obtain adequate clothing or you have a closet filled with more than you could wear, God knows that you need clothes, and it is He who provides them for you. Thank Him now for clothing you throughout your life.

GOD, YOU WANT ME TO KNOW THAT . . .

YOU SATISFY MY HUNGER AND THIRST

[The Lord] provides food for those who fear Him. (PSALM 111:5)

[Jesus taught us to pray,] "Give us each day our daily bread." (LUKE 11:3)

Related verses: Psalm 23:2, 5; 107:9; Ecclesiastes 9:7; Matthew 6:11, 26, 31–33; Luke 12:24.

Some make a regular practice of giving thanks to God at meals. Perhaps you do as well. Explore before your Lord the purpose and value of doing so.

GOD, YOU WANT ME TO KNOW THAT . . .

YOU ADDRESS MY LIFE AND HEALTH

Bless the Lord, O my soul, and forget not all His benefits, who forgives all your iniquity, who heals all your diseases, who redeems your life from the pit, who crowns you with steadfast love and mercy, who satisfies you with good so that your youth is renewed like the eagle's. (PSALM 103:2–5)

Related verses: Exodus 15:26; Deuteronomy 30:20; Psalm 41:3; 91:16; 127:2; Ezekiel 34:15; Matthew 8:17.

Acknowledge to your Lord the role He plays in your health and healing. Praise Him for the times you have witnessed healing at His gracious hand.

GOD, YOU WANT ME TO KNOW THAT . . .

YOU BLESS MY HOME

[The Lord] blesses the dwelling of the righteous. (PROVERBS 3:33)

Related verse: Luke 10:5.

Have you ever held or attended a house-blessing ceremony? Describe to the Lord what it means for you to know that He Himself blesses your home.

50

Filled with the Fullness of God

I recall once attempting to double the recipe for a batch of brownies. I am still not fully certain what happened, but I know the result was definitely *not* brownies. God unfailingly follows His recipe for growing and maturing you. When God fills you with His fullness, He never gives you less than the full portion. The bread of life and living water that He provides is always more than enough. He gives all of Himself to you so that the finished product is exactly what He promises. In the hands of the Master Baker, you are coming out just right!

GOD, YOU WANT ME TO KNOW THAT . . .

YOU ENABLE ME TO SHARE IN YOUR SON

We have come to share in Christ. (HEBREWS 3:14)

For this reason I bow my knees before the Father, . . . that according to the riches of His glory He may grant you to be strengthened with power through His Spirit in your inner being, *so that Christ may dwell in your hearts through faith . . . that you may be filled with all the fullness of God.* (EPHESIANS 3:14, 16–17, 19)

Related verse: Philemon 6.

Sharing in Christ involves participating in Him and in all that belongs to Him. Present your thoughts to Jesus about what this might encompass in your life.

GOD, YOU WANT ME TO KNOW THAT . . .

YOU GIVE ME LIVING WATER

[Jesus said,] "Whoever believes in Me, as the Scripture has said, 'Out of his heart will flow rivers of living water.'" (JOHN 7:38)

Related verses: Psalm 36:9; Isaiah 58:11; John 4:14.

While the woman at the well was getting her daily bucket of water, Jesus offered her ***living water*** (John 4:7–15). Think about spiritual satisfaction, the gift of the Holy Spirit, and the waters of Baptism. Consider with Jesus how you might explain ***living water*** to a friend using your own words.

GOD, YOU WANT ME TO KNOW THAT . . .

YOU GIVE ME THE BREAD OF LIFE

Jesus said to them, "I am the bread of life; whoever comes to Me shall not hunger, and whoever believes in Me shall never thirst." (JOHN 6:35)

Related verses: Luke 22:19; John 6:35–40, 48–51, 53–58.

Like water, food is essential to life. Jesus identified Himself as the bread of life. Think about sustaining life, spiritual nutrition, and the source of vitality. Recognize with Jesus how He is the bread of life for you.

51

Given Every Good Gift

What is your love language? God is fluent in them all! When it comes to gift-giving, no one can compare. He's absolutely in a league of His own. He gives abundantly, consistently, and irrevocably. He keeps His promises without fail. He gives you rest from the impossible demands of the Law. He provides times of refreshing for you. He honors and exalts you. What surprise token of His love is on its way to you this very day? I'll bet you can't wait to find out!

GOD, YOU WANT ME TO KNOW THAT . . .

YOU GIVE ME YOUR GIFTS

Every good gift and every perfect gift is from above, coming down from the Father of lights, with whom there is no variation or shadow due to change. (JAMES 1:17)

Related verses: Matthew 7:11; Ephesians 4:7.

Present to your Father a list of several of His wonderful gifts to you. Contrast these to the counterfeit gifts that the sinful world offers.

GOD, YOU WANT ME TO KNOW THAT . . .

I EXPERIENCE YOUR REST

[Jesus said,] "*Come to Me, all who labor and are heavy laden, and I will give you rest.* Take My yoke upon you, and learn from Me, for I am gentle and lowly in heart, and *you will find rest for your souls. For My yoke is easy, and My burden is light.*" (MATTHEW 11:28–30)

Related verses: Psalm 4:1; Hebrews 4:1, 3, 9–10.

Here Jesus contrasts the frustrating and burdensome legalism of the Pharisees with the grace and forgiveness that He offers through faith in Him. Jesus kept the Law perfectly in your place. If your soul is enjoying Jesus' wonderful rest, thank Him now. If not, ask God to help you learn about and fully experience this rest.

GOD, YOU WANT ME TO KNOW THAT . . .

YOU HONOR AND EXALT ME

[The Lord declares,] "I will be with him in trouble; I will rescue him and honor him." (PSALM 91:15)

[The Lord] has brought down the mighty from their thrones and *exalted those of humble estate.* (LUKE 1:52)

Related verses: 1 Chronicles 29:12; Psalm 37:34; 89:16; 2 Corinthians 8:9; 1 Peter 5:6.

You instinctively recognize that you deserve God's rejection and wrath. React before God to the news that He intends to honor you as His friend and to exalt you in the sight of all.

I AM BLESSED TO SERVE

With the prospect of perfect joy in heaven, why in the world are you still here in the world? It's because God still has important work for you to do here!

52

Given Purpose

You have been commissioned to carry on God's gracious work on earth—to lead others to Him and to help and support your brothers and sisters in Christ. He has enough confidence in you (actually, in Himself) that He entrusts you with carrying out His plan of extending the reach of His love and kindness here.

GOD, YOU WANT ME TO KNOW THAT . . .

YOU GIVE ME PURPOSE

I cry out to God Most High, to God who fulfills His purpose for me. (PSALM 57:2)

Related verses: Psalm 138:8; Jeremiah 29:11; Romans 8:28; 11:29.

Express your amazement to God Most High that He carries out His plans and purposes for you in your life. Ponder with Him what those plans and purposes might entail.

GOD, YOU WANT ME TO KNOW THAT . . .

I AM SERVING YOU

Whatever you do, work heartily, as for the Lord and not for men, knowing that from the Lord you will receive the inheritance as your reward. *You are serving the Lord Christ.* (COLOSSIANS 3:23–24)

Related verses: Isaiah 41:9; Mark 8:35; Romans 7:6; 1 Corinthians 15:58; Philemon 6.

Most people probably recognize that Christian pastors, teachers, and missionaries are full-time servants of God. But did you realize you are also His full-time servant? Talk with Him about what this implies for you.

GOD, YOU WANT ME TO KNOW THAT . . .

YOU HAVE DESIGNATED ME YOUR STEWARD

As each has received a gift, use it to serve one another, as good stewards of God's varied grace. (1 PETER 4:10)

Related verses: Psalm 8:6–8; Matthew 25:14–17, 21, 29.

How many sheets of notebook paper would it take to list everything you own? Answer: zero! God owns it all. We are His caretakers, or stewards. Explore with God how this truth might change the way you think and operate each day and how acknowledging this reality can be freeing.

53

Productive Life

One morning as I walked around the street corner, I discovered that my neighbor's massive tree had been uprooted by strong winds during the night and was now lying on the ground. The roots that once anchored the tree and provided it with water and nourishment were now exposed. I knew that all its green leaves would soon turn brown and fall off. What a chilling image of life apart from Christ! But in Christ, you are like a tree securely planted by a constant water source. You are enabled to produce an abundance of fruit—serving and blessing others. And Jesus, your master gardener, is always helping you to bear even more fruit.

GOD, YOU WANT ME TO KNOW THAT . . .

YOU APPOINT ME TO BEAR FRUIT

[Jesus said,] "You did not choose Me, but I chose you and appointed you that you should go and bear fruit and that your fruit should abide." (JOHN 15:16)

Blessed is the man who trusts in the LORD. . . . He is like a tree planted by water, that sends out its roots by the stream, and does not fear when heat comes, for its leaves remain green, and is not anxious in the year of drought, for it does not cease to bear fruit. (JEREMIAH 17:7-8)

[The righteous] still bear fruit in old age; they are ever full of sap and green, to declare that the LORD is upright. (PSALM 92:14-15)

Related verses: Psalm 1:3; Isaiah 27:6; Ezekiel 34:26; Matthew 13:23; John 15:2, 5; Romans 7:4.

✎ **In the Bible, fruit represents everything you do in partnership with Jesus Christ. Consider with Jesus what it means to you that He appoints you to bear fruit and how this happens.**

GOD, YOU WANT ME TO KNOW THAT . . .

YOUR SPIRIT PRODUCES HIS FRUIT IN ME

But the fruit of the Spirit is love, joy, peace, patience, kindness, goodness, faithfulness, gentleness, self-control; against such things there is no law. (GALATIANS 5:22–23)

But now that you have been set free from sin and have become slaves of God, the fruit you get leads to sanctification and its end, eternal life. (ROMANS 6:22)

Related verses: John 14:27; Romans 8:6; 14:17; Ephesians 3:17; 4:1–3; Philippians 4:7; Colossians 1:11; 3:12, 14; 1 Thessalonians 5:23; 2 Timothy 1:7.

✎ **The fruit of the Spirit is the personality of Jesus Christ Himself, at times evidenced in your life as God's beloved child. Note that none of the fruit that the Holy Spirit produces in you can be fully expressed apart from other people. Reflect with the Spirit on the following statement: True Christian faith is always personal but never private.**

54

God Working through Me

As my wife and I walked up to the hospital where my daughter was to be born, I was shocked by the massive wooden front doors. I wondered aloud, "How could a sick person ever get into this place?" But when I reached to open the door, it swung open easily with the help of a power-assist motor. This is similar to what happens when you act in faith on God's commands. The works that God wants you to accomplish may seem daunting, but the power of the Holy Spirit within you enables you to carry out whatever He asks of you. He chooses good works for you to do, He prepares them in advance, He creates in you the desire to do them, and He Himself does them through you. So don't be afraid to reach out and open that door!

GOD, YOU WANT ME TO KNOW THAT . . .

YOUR SON CONTINUES HIS WORK THROUGH ME

[Jesus said,] "Truly, truly, I say to you, whoever believes in Me will also do the works that I do; and greater works than these will he do, because I am going to the Father." (JOHN 14:12)

Related verses: Matthew 5:13–14; Ephesians 5:8.

How could it possibly be that we will do greater works than Jesus did? Our minds might jump to miraculous signs and wonders, but the chief work of Jesus was to lay down His life for the world He loves and to lead people to believe in Him (John 3:16). As a member of Jesus' church throughout the world, recognize before Him the incredible opportunity you have to participate in His work of loving people (Matthew 22:39) and introducing them to Him (Matthew 28:18–20).

GOD, YOU WANT ME TO KNOW THAT . . .

YOU ENABLE ME TO DO GOOD WORKS

We are [God's] workmanship, created in Christ Jesus for good works, which God prepared beforehand, that we should walk in them. (EPHESIANS 2:10)

It is God who works in you, both to will and to work for His good pleasure. (PHILIPPIANS 2:13)

Related verses: Isaiah 26:12; 1 Corinthians 15:58; 2 Corinthians 9:8; 2 Thessalonians 1:11; 2:16–17; 2 Timothy 3:16–17; Titus 2:14; Hebrews 13:20–21.

Summarize for God how He participates in your good works and why that is a very good thing.

55

His Power at Work in Me

During a power failure in your home, your microwave becomes just another cabinet and your TV a rather poor mirror. They only fulfill their intended purposes when plugged into a live power source. I've heard Christians talk about their need to "recharge their spiritual batteries." By attending the vital gift of Sunday morning worship and perhaps a nourishing midweek service or Bible study, they hope to store up enough power to function through the rest of the week. But one day, as I was meditating on John 15:5, where Jesus declares that apart from Him we can do *nothing*, I realized that you and I don't have batteries! Power only flows through us as we are connected to *Him*, our power source. In Christ, we are given unlimited access to God's limitless power at all times—the very same power that raised Jesus from the dead! And by God's grace, we remain securely plugged in.

GOD, YOU WANT ME TO KNOW THAT . . .

YOU CLOTHE ME WITH POWER

I do not cease to give thanks for you, remembering you in my prayers, . . . having the eyes of your hearts enlightened, that you may know . . . *the immeasurable greatness of* [*God's*] *power toward us who believe*, according to the working of His great might that He worked in Christ when He raised Him from the dead and seated Him at His right hand in the heavenly places. (EPHESIANS 1:16, 18, 19–20)

Related verses: Psalm 18:32; 68:35; Luke 24:49; 1 Corinthians 1:24; 2 Corinthians 12:9; Ephesians 3:20; Philippians 3:10; 2 Timothy 1:7.

Marvel with God about the amazing fact that the very same power He used to raise Jesus Christ from the dead is now at work in you.

GOD, YOU WANT ME TO KNOW THAT . . .

THE GIFT OF YOUR HOLY SPIRIT EMPOWERS ME

For this reason I bow my knees before the Father, . . . that according to the riches of His glory He may grant you to be strengthened with power through His Spirit in your inner being. (EPHESIANS 3:14, 16)

Related verses: Isaiah 44:3; Ezekiel 39:29; Matthew 3:11; Luke 24:49; Acts 2:16–18, 38–39; Romans 5:5; 1 Corinthians 2:12; 2 Corinthians 1:21; 1 John 3:24.

Thank your Father that He empowers you through the presence of His Holy Spirit within you.

GOD, YOU WANT ME TO KNOW THAT . . .

YOU UNIQUELY EQUIP ME TO SERVE OTHERS

Having gifts that differ according to the grace given to us, let us use them. (ROMANS 12:6)

As each has received a gift, use it to serve one another, as good stewards of God's varied grace. (1 PETER 4:10)

Related verses: Romans 11:29; 1 Corinthians 7:7; 12:7.

Identify with God some specific gifts He has given to you that enable you to serve others. Share with Him the joy and blessings you experience in sharing such gifts.

GOD, YOU WANT ME TO KNOW THAT . . .

YOU ENABLE ME TO DO ALL THINGS

God is able to make all grace abound to you, so that *having all sufficiency in all things at all times, you may abound in every good work.* (2 CORINTHIANS 9:8)

I have learned in whatever situation I am to be content. I know how to be brought low, and I know how to abound. . . . *I can do all things through Him who strengthens me.* (PHILIPPIANS 4:11–13)

Related verses: Mark 9:23; 2 Corinthians 13:3.

There is essentially no limit to what God can accomplish in and through you. Recall with Him a situation or two in which, without His gracious involvement, you could never have accomplished a project that He inspired or faced a difficult situation that He allowed.

56

Worshiping in Spirit and Truth

You were created, redeemed, and empowered so that God is glorified in you and your life. Worship and praise are your expressions of love and appreciation to your wonderful God, who loves you and gave His Son for you. You join freely and gladly in worship with your brothers and sisters in Christ. He fills you with songs of praise and thanksgiving, and you sing for joy (or at least make a "joyful noise"). You share Christ's wondrous meal, to which He personally invites you. All of these are but a wonderful foretaste of the ultimate worship, the glorious music, and the heavenly banquet yet to come!

GOD, YOU WANT ME TO KNOW THAT

YOU ENABLE ME TO WORSHIP GENUINELY

The hour is coming, and is now here, when the true worshipers will worship the Father in spirit and truth. (JOHN 4:23)

Related verses: Psalm 22:3; John 4:24; Ephesians 1:3–14; 3:20–21; Hebrews 12:28; 1 Peter 2:5.

The word *worship* is a shortened form of the Old English word *worthscip*—the idea of someone or something having worth. Express to the Father several facts about Him that make Him totally worthy of your adoration, devotion, and praise.

GOD, YOU WANT ME TO KNOW THAT

YOU GIVE ME SONGS OF PRAISE

[*The Lord*] *put a new song in my mouth, a song of praise to our God.* Many will see and fear, and put their trust in the Lord. (PSALM 40:3)

Be filled with the Spirit, addressing one another in psalms and hymns and spiritual songs, singing and making melody to the Lord with your heart. (EPHESIANS 5:18–19)

Related verses: Exodus 15:2; Job 35:10; Psalm 63:7; 118:14.

Songs, hymns, and spiritual songs are useful for addressing your Lord, for encouraging fellow believers, and for reaching out to unbelievers. Recount to your Lord Jesus Christ occasions when you have personally experienced these three uses.

GOD, YOU WANT ME TO KNOW THAT

YOUR SON INVITES ME TO HIS SUPPER

I received from the Lord what I also delivered to you, that the Lord Jesus on the night when He was betrayed took bread, and when He had given thanks, He broke it, and said, *"This is My body, which is for you. Do this in remembrance of Me."* In the same way also He took the cup, after supper, saying, *"This cup is the new covenant in My blood. Do this, as often as you drink it, in remembrance of Me."* For as often as you eat this bread and drink the cup, you proclaim the Lord's death until He comes. (1 CORINTHIANS 11:23–26)

Related verses: Isaiah 26:3; Matthew 26:26–28; Romans 8:6.

Identify before Christ your Lord reasons why you participate in His Supper and the blessings you receive as a result.

In his second letter, Peter emphasized God's "precious and very great promises" and expressed his intent that "you may be able at any time to recall these things" (1:4, 15). So far, we have explored and taken personally God's promises and assurances for both *yesterday* and *today*. But your journey would not be complete without also visiting God's promises and assurances that are yet to be realized. The following *forever* part of this trip might very well be my favorite, and I am honored to have you along. Marvel and enjoy!

FOREVER

That you may know . . . what are the riches of [God's] glorious inheritance in the saints.

EPHESIANS 1:18

During tough or disappointing situations, I like to share two things that I know for sure: (1) I am going to heaven, and (2) this isn't it. Outside of funerals, most people don't talk much about death and heaven. The first-century world Jesus entered wasn't much different. But Jesus extensively interjected into His conversations with people the topics of death, His return, and the life to come. You will find Him addressing such topics in over a third of the red-letter verses in the Gospel of Matthew and in nearly half of all His recorded parables.

As real and tangible as this physical universe is, Jesus reminds you that it is temporary. Instead of loving the world and the things in it, His earnest desire is for you to set your heart instead on the things above. Because of infection with sin, all creation groans as it eagerly awaits our transformation at Christ's return and the revealing of the new heavens and new earth.

In your journey through God's remarkable promises and assurances, you have seen God's faithfulness both *yesterday* and *today.* By the working of God's Spirit, you are enabled to have the same confidence in the promises and assurances yet to be fulfilled. In the following pages, you will review all God has revealed to you about the perfect, sin-free kingdom that awaits. Each day brings you closer to experiencing all He has promised you. It could be today!

HOPE THAT DOESN'T DISAPPOINT

You probably know what it is like to be let down by someone you trusted. You feel so hurt and violated. God offers you a very different kind of hope. He has demonstrated His perfect faithfulness so that you are learning to trust Him unconditionally. You can be equally confident about all He promises regarding the future. Though all others fail you, God cannot and will not!

57

The Hope That Is in Me

We often use the word *hope* casually today, like wishing ("I hope the rain holds off") or politely asking ("I hope you don't mind"). But in the Bible, *hope* refers to confident, bet-your-life expectation for a future event or situation. As a believer, your life is based on and defined by hope—hope for forgiveness, hope for redemption, hope for access to heaven. God's Word proclaims these precious promises, and the Holy Spirit enables you to rely upon them. The Lord has repeatedly proven to you His faithfulness, and He has given you His Holy Spirit as a pledge of assurance that all of His wonderful promises to you will be perfectly fulfilled.

GOD, YOU WANT ME TO KNOW THAT . . .

YOU PROVIDE ME HOPE

For God alone, O my soul, wait in silence, for *my hope is from Him.* (PSALM 62:5)

Hope does not put us to shame, because God's love has been poured into our hearts through the Holy Spirit who has been given to us. (ROMANS 5:5)

Related verses: Jeremiah 14:8; Lamentations 3:24; Matthew 12:21; Romans 5:2; 10:11; 15:13; 2 Thessalonians 2:16; Titus 3:7; 1 Peter 1:21.

Trace for God the basis of your hope in Him and how you can be absolutely confident in that hope.

GOD, YOU WANT ME TO KNOW THAT . . .

YOU HAVE ENROLLED ME IN HEAVEN

But you have come to Mount Zion and to the city of the living God, the heavenly Jerusalem, . . . and to *the assembly of the firstborn who are enrolled in heaven.* (HEBREWS 12:22–23)

Related verses: Luke 10:20; Philippians 3:20.

Reflect with God on how your citizenship in heaven bolsters your hope for the future and impacts your life here today.

GOD, YOU WANT ME TO KNOW THAT . . .

YOU GUARANTEE MY INHERITANCE

You also were included in Christ when you heard the message of truth, the gospel of your salvation. When you believed, *you were marked in Him with a seal, the promised Holy Spirit, who is a deposit guaranteeing our inheritance* until the redemption of those who are God's possession—to the praise of His glory. (EPHESIANS 1:13–14 NIV)

Related verses: Matthew 5:3, 5; Luke 12:32; 2 Corinthians 1:22; Ephesians 1:18; Hebrews 1:14; 10:34; 1 Peter 1:3–4.

As part of the Bride of Christ, His beloved church, suggest how the Holy Spirit might be compared to an engagement ring. Glorify God for sealing His commitment to you with His Holy Spirit.

58

Endless Confidence

Will you make it to heaven? What if you don't remain faithful to the end? What if you fall short, losing interest or focus? If the outcome depended entirely on *you*, your prospects would indeed be bleak. But since your hope is in *Christ*, you are completely secure, because *He* is perfectly dependable. It's not that someday you will enter eternal life—you're already there! Because *He* is mighty and faithful, you can have unwavering confidence.

GOD, YOU WANT ME TO KNOW THAT . . .

YOU'LL SUSTAIN ME TO THE END

Now may the God of peace Himself sanctify you completely, and may your whole spirit and soul and body be kept blameless at the coming of our Lord Jesus Christ. He who calls you is faithful; He will surely do it. (1 THESSALONIANS 5:23–24)

Related verses: Romans 6:22; 1 Corinthians 1:8; 15:57; Galatians 6:8; Philippians 1:6; 1 Peter 1:5, 7; 1 John 4:17; Jude 24.

Most of us could probably start a marathon, but finishing one is quite a different matter. Consider with the God of peace how you can be sure that you will remain faithful to the end and be confident on "the day of judgment" (1 John 4:17).

GOD, YOU WANT ME TO KNOW THAT . . .

MY ETERNAL LIFE HAS ALREADY BEGUN

[Jesus said,] "Truly, truly, I say to you, whoever hears My word and believes Him who sent Me has eternal life." (JOHN 5:24)

We know that we have passed out of death into life. (1 JOHN 3:14)

Related verses: John 3:36; 4:14; 6:51; 10:28–29; 11:25–26; 1 Timothy 6:12.

Tell your Lord what it means to you that your eternal life has already begun.

59

Awaiting with Eager Anticipation

Most of us typically live and function in the present. But sometimes you may be looking forward to a special event—perhaps a wedding, a reunion, or a once-in-a-lifetime trip. As you wait and anticipate, you still perform your everyday tasks and activities. But the upcoming event impacts your mood, thoughts, and perspective. You may walk with an extra spring in your step. You enjoy looking forward to this event in conversations with others who are also looking forward to it. How much more can you anticipate life eternal—walking with God in the new perfect heavens and earth and experiencing absolute joy!

ASSURED BY YOUR PROMISES, GOD, . . .

I EAGERLY AWAIT YOUR SON'S RETURN

Christ, having been offered once to bear the sins of many, will appear a second time, not to deal with sin but *to save those who are eagerly waiting for Him.* (HEBREWS 9:28)

Related verses: Matthew 24:42; Philippians 3:20; 1 Thessalonians 1:10; 5:2, 4.

Summarize for Jesus what wonderful changes you expect to be ushered in when He returns in glory.

ASSURED BY YOUR PROMISES, GOD, . . .

I EAGERLY AWAIT YOUR FULL SALVATION

It will be said on that day, "Behold, this is our God; we have waited for Him, that He might save us. This is the LORD; we have waited for Him; let us be glad and rejoice in His salvation." (ISAIAH 25:9)

Related verses: Isaiah 56:1; Zechariah 9:16; Matthew 24:13; Acts 2:21; 15:11; Philippians 3:20; Hebrews 7:25; 1 Peter 1:9.

List for God several things that you look forward to being saved from. Contemplate what full salvation might look and feel like.

ASSURED BY YOUR PROMISES, GOD, . . .

I EAGERLY AWAIT YOUR RIGHTEOUSNESS

Through the Spirit, by faith, we ourselves eagerly wait for the hope of righteousness. (GALATIANS 5:5)

In keeping with [God's] promise we are looking forward to a new heaven and a new earth, *where righteousness dwells.* (2 PETER 3:13 NIV)

Related verses: Isaiah 62:1; Matthew 5:6.

Acknowledge to God various aspects of your life today that might lead you to eagerly await perfect righteousness—where no more sin, wickedness, or evil will be present.

ASSURED BY YOUR PROMISES, GOD, . . .

I EAGERLY AWAIT HEAVEN

According to [God's] promise *we are waiting for new heavens and a new earth* in which righteousness dwells. (2 PETER 3:13)

Related verses: Isaiah 65:17; 2 Corinthians 4:17–18; 1 Peter 5:10; Revelation 21:2.

Jesus shared a parable in Luke 14:16–24. Here, people who were invited to a great banquet (heaven) made excuses for why they couldn't attend, such as needing to inspect recently purchased real estate or livestock or having been newly married. Honestly admit things about your life now that might be dampening your enthusiasm about the life to come. Confess these before God and pray for an increasingly eager anticipation of your amazing home in the new creation.

60

Waiting to Be Changed

A few Thanksgivings ago, I was playing touch football with my sons-in-law and their brothers and friends. After repeatedly finding myself on the ground, I came to the brilliant conclusion that I should probably retire from playing football. Perhaps you are now young and vital, but you know such things are liable to change over time. Today I can enjoy a fifteen-mile walk, but in the future, it may be a major accomplishment for me to get to the mailbox and back. In this fallen world, perhaps you entered life with a disability or have since been diagnosed with a chronic condition. Regardless, everyone who is in Christ has this fact in common: we shall all be changed (1 Corinthians 15:51). You will be getting a new, glorified body like the body of the resurrected Christ! How amazing is that?

GOD, YOU WANT ME TO KNOW THAT . . .

YOU WILL TRANSFORM MY BODY

We know that if the tent that is our earthly home is destroyed, *we have a building from God, a house not made with hands, eternal in the heavens.* For in this tent we groan, *longing to put on our heavenly dwelling,* if indeed by putting it on we may not be found naked. For while we are still in this tent, we groan, being burdened—not that we would be unclothed, but that *we would be further clothed, so that what is mortal may be swallowed up by life. He who has prepared us for this very thing is God, who has given us the Spirit as a guarantee.*

(2 CORINTHIANS 5:1–5)

Related verses: Romans 8:23; 1 Corinthians 15:35, 42–49, 51–52; 1 John 3:2.

Identify some physical limitations or deterioration you have experienced. Envision with God what will be different once you receive your renewed, glorified body in heaven.

GOD, YOU WANT ME TO KNOW THAT . . .

YOU WILL PERFECT MY MIND AND SPIRIT

Now I know in part; then I shall know fully, even as I have been fully known. (1 CORINTHIANS 13:12)

You have come . . . to God, the judge of all, and *to the spirits of the righteous made perfect.* (HEBREWS 12:22–23)

Related verses: 1 Corinthians 13:10; Philippians 4:7.

We have all experienced moments of mental fog or times when our memory fails us. Meditate before God what it will mean to have a mind that knows fully and a spirit or heart that has been made perfect.

MY IMMINENT DEPARTURE

One of my favorite single-frame comics shows a man looking at the western sky from his porch, and superimposed on the sunset are the words "THE END," like one might see at the end of a classic movie. He calls into the house, "Edith, come quick!" One day soon, whether through your death or through Christ's return to earth in glory, this comic will become your reality!

61

Regarding Physical Death

The phrase "If I should die before I wake, I pray the Lord my soul to take" was a part of my bedtime prayer as a child. Early on, I simply learned to recite these words, but eventually, it hit me: wait, could that actually happen? Though you might not usually give it much thought, you would have to agree that today could be your last day on earth. A car accident, a heart attack, or any number of causes could suddenly bring your life on earth to a close. Since Christ was raised from the dead, however, you can be certain that you will likewise rise, and your death will prove to be your portal into Christ's presence. And after that, you can never and will never die again!

GOD, YOU WANT ME TO KNOW THAT . . .

YOU HAVE SCHEDULED MY HOMECOMING

[Man's] days are determined, and the number of his months is with You, and You have appointed his limits that he cannot pass. (JOB 14:5)

Precious in the sight of the LORD is the death of His saints. (PSALM 116:15)

Related verses: Psalm 37:18; 139:16; Luke 23:43; Revelation 14:13.

Today you are one day closer to your heavenly homecoming. The Lord your God has that day circled on His calendar. Share your reaction to this image with Him.

GOD, YOU WANT ME TO KNOW THAT . . .

MY DEATH IS SWALLOWED UP IN VICTORY

When the perishable puts on the imperishable, and the mortal puts on immortality, then shall come to pass the saying that is written: "Death is swallowed up in victory." (1 CORINTHIANS 15:54)

Related verses: Isaiah 25:8; John 3:16; 1 Corinthians 15:53–57; 2 Timothy 1:10.

The curse for sinning is death. Unless Jesus returns first, you will most certainly die someday. But now that you belong to Christ, point out to Him several ways that death is different for you.

GOD, YOU WANT ME TO KNOW THAT . . .

I CAN'T DIE AGAIN

They cannot die anymore*, because they are equal to angels and are sons of God, *being sons of the resurrection. (LUKE 20:36)

Related verses: John 11:25–26; Revelation 2:11; 21:4.

Although your days are indeed numbered on earth, there will be no final day in heaven. Take some time exploring before God what that means to you.

62

I Will See Christ Coming

One time I packed up the family and set out to view a total solar eclipse. After weeks of preparation—ordering special glasses, finding the best viewing sites, and monitoring the weather—we were able to marvel at the darkened sun surrounded by its glowing corona. Birds went silent, and the locusts began singing. It was an unforgettable spectacle! But there is another heavenly show that could occur at any moment, the likes of which has never before been seen. Christ will return in great power and glory, and for all those "who have loved His appearing" (2 Timothy 4:8), it will be a time of unimaginable joy! And all will see it with their own eyes—no special glasses required.

GOD, YOU WANT ME TO KNOW THAT . . .

YOUR SON IS COMING FOR ME

Again the high priest asked Him, "Are You the Christ, the Son of the Blessed?" And Jesus said, "I am, and *you will see the Son of Man seated at the right hand of Power, and coming with the clouds of heaven.*" (MARK 14:61–62)

Related verses: Job 19:25; Matthew 26:63–64.

Imagine you are sitting on a patio chair or driving down a highway when the sky in front of you splits open and the Lord Jesus suddenly appears in glory with legions of angels. Describe to Him both the scene and your reactions to it.

GOD, YOU WANT ME TO KNOW THAT . . .

YOUR SON WILL GATHER ME WITH HIS ELECT

[The Son of Man] will send out His angels with a loud trumpet call, and they will gather His elect from the four winds, from one end of heaven to the other. (MATTHEW 24:31)

Related verses: Psalm 73:24; Matthew 3:12; Mark 13:27.

Don't worry if you are out of town, on vacation, or orbiting earth in the International Space Station. Envision before Jesus, the Son of Man, what being gathered together with all believers from every place might be like.

GOD, YOU WANT ME TO KNOW . . .

WHAT WILL HAPPEN IF I'VE ALREADY DIED

Since we believe that Jesus died and rosc again, even so, through Jesus, *God will bring with Him those who have fallen asleep.* (1 THESSALONIANS 4:14)

The Lord Himself will descend from heaven with a cry of command, with the voice of an archangel, and with the sound of the trumpet of God. And the dead in Christ will rise first. (1 THESSALONIANS 4:16)

[God] who raised the Lord Jesus will raise us also with Jesus and bring us with you into His presence. (2 CORINTHIANS 4:14)

Related verses: Isaiah 26:19; Daniel 12:2; John 6:39–40, 54; Romans 6:5; 1 Corinthians 15:20–23, 54; Philippians 3:10–11.

Fallen asleep **is an expression meaning "died," which recognizes that each believer will one day "awaken" to**

eternal life at Christ's return. Based on these verses, summarize what you will experience on that day if you have already died.

GOD, YOU WANT ME TO KNOW . . .

WHAT WILL HAPPEN IF I'M STILL ALIVE

This we declare to you by a word from the Lord, that *we who are alive, who are left until the coming of the Lord, will not precede those who have fallen asleep.* (1 THESSALONIANS 4:15)

Then we who are alive, who are left, will be caught up together with them in the clouds to meet the Lord in the air, and so we will always be with the Lord. (1 THESSALONIANS 4:17)

Related verses: Luke 21:5–36; John 16:13; 1 Corinthians 15:51–52; Revelation 1:1.

Based on these verses, summarize what events will take place if you are still alive on the day when your Lord returns.

ALWAYS WITH THE LORD

Eternity is a really hard concept to wrap our finite minds around. What will you be doing forever? Could you ever tire of it? Not in the least! Let's explore some of the promises about you being forever with the Lord.

63

I Will Enter the Kingdom of Heaven

You are on the honored guest list, and the door of God's kingdom swings wide open. Jesus has completed your room with all the special touches He knows will communicate to you how very much He loves you. There you are welcomed by your amazing God—Father, Son, and Holy Spirit. And if that weren't enough, you get to enjoy talking with saints throughout the ages, including Noah, Abraham, Ruth, David, Isaiah, Esther, Mary, the Gospel writers, the apostle Paul, and the list goes on and on. And they will be just as excited to meet you and enjoy your story! You don't have to fumble for a ticket or pull up an app on your phone—you are recognized immediately and lovingly ushered in.

GOD, YOU WANT ME TO KNOW THAT . . .

YOU WILL AUTHORIZE MY ENTRY

In this way there will be richly provided for you an entrance into the eternal kingdom of our Lord and Savior Jesus Christ. (2 PETER 1:11)

Related verses: Zechariah 8:8; Revelation 22:14.

Forget the jokes about having to get past a stern apostle Peter at heaven's gates. Instead, reflect with your Lord and Savior Jesus Christ on what it means that an entrance into His eternal kingdom has been richly provided for you.

GOD, YOU WANT ME TO KNOW THAT . . .

YOUR SON WILL HAVE A PLACE PREPARED FOR ME

[Jesus said,] "In My Father's house are many rooms. If it were not so, would I have told you that I go to prepare a place for you? And if I go and prepare a place for you, I will come again and will take you to Myself, that where I am you may be also." (JOHN 14:2–3)

Related verses: 1 Chronicles 17:9; Psalm 23:6; Ezekiel 37:27; 2 Timothy 2:11; Hebrews 11:16; Revelation 21:3.

Visualize and share with Jesus what you anticipate your prepared place might be like.

GOD, YOU WANT ME TO KNOW THAT . . .

WE WILL CELEBRATE TOGETHER

The angel said to me, "Write this: *Blessed are those who are invited to the marriage supper of the Lamb.*" And he said to me, "These are the true words of God." (REVELATION 19:9)

People will come from east and west, and from north and south, and recline at table in the kingdom of God. (LUKE 13:29)

Related verses: Matthew 8:11; 26:29; Luke 22:30; Revelation 2:17; 22:3.

Bring to mind the most memorable celebration you have been privileged to attend so far. At the marriage supper mentioned here, Jesus welcomes His Bride, the church, to heaven. Talk with God about this unprecedented occasion.

GOD, YOU WANT ME TO KNOW THAT . . .

YOU WILL RESTORE TO US ONE COMMON LANGUAGE

[The Lord declares,] "For at that time I will change the speech of the peoples to a pure speech, that all of them may call upon the name of the LORD and serve Him with one accord." (ZEPHANIAH 3:9)

Related verses: Genesis 11:1–9; Acts 2:4–11; Revelation 5:9; 7:9.

At Babel, the one common language of Eden was shattered into differing languages and scrambled communication. In heaven, one common language will at last be restored. Contemplate with the Lord what differences this will make for you.

64

God's Wrath Will Be Fully Satisfied

In God's forever kingdom, His wrath against sin has been fully appeased. Sin has no hold over anyone there, and the fruit of the Spirit holds full sway. Nothing remains to obscure God's amazing love, and nothing hinders you from seeing God face to face. Only those who by faith have received the salvation that Christ purchased for them are now present. Welcome to complete access and perfect acceptance!

GOD, YOU WANT ME TO KNOW THAT . . .

YOU WILL NOT CONDEMN ME

For God did not send His Son into the world to condemn the world, but in order that the world might be saved through Him. Whoever believes in Him is not condemned. (JOHN 3:17–18)

Related verses: John 5:24; Romans 8:1–2; 1 Peter 1:13.

Do you have any anxiety about being presented before the holy, almighty God when Jesus returns? Consider with Jesus, God's only Son, what it means for you that there will definitely be no condemnation and why that is true for you.

GOD, YOU WANT ME TO KNOW THAT . . .

YOUR WRATH AGAINST MY SIN WILL BE SATISFIED

Since, therefore, we have now been justified by [Christ's] blood, *much more shall we be saved by Him from the wrath of God.* (ROMANS 5:9)

Related verses: Leviticus 26:11; Hosea 11:9; 14:4; 1 Thessalonians 1:10; 5:9–10.

Today, many downplay uncomfortable messages about God's wrath and hell. Thank God that these very real matters will not be a part of your eternal future.

GOD, YOU WANT ME TO KNOW THAT . . .

YOU WILL JUDGE MY ENEMIES

God considers it just to repay with affliction those who afflict you, and to grant relief to you who are afflicted as well as to us, when the Lord Jesus is revealed from heaven with His mighty angels in flaming fire. (2 THESSALONIANS 1:6–8)

Related verses: Psalm 145:20; Matthew 13:49–50; Luke 13:27–28; John 3:36; 5:28–29; Galatians 5:19–21; 6:7; Hebrews 10:31; Revelation 20:14–15.

Like God, we are to take no joy in the death of the wicked. At the same time, explore with Him what assurance you find here about His justice, holiness, and integrity.

65

I Will Be in His Presence

Yes, you have already been adopted, but now you finally get to move in to your new, permanent home. Talk about a desirable neighborhood! Describe your perfect home, including the amenities, features, recreation, and stunning view. Can you picture it in your mind? Well, that's not even close to what it will be like. Scripture tells us no one can even *imagine* what God has prepared for those He loves—it will be that much better! And however wonderful heaven will be—and it will be wonderful, to be sure—it all pales in comparison to the joy of being in the Lord's presence face to face, fully experiencing His perfect love for you.

GOD, YOU WANT ME TO KNOW THAT . . .

YOU WILL ENHANCE MY ADOPTION

Not only the creation, but *we ourselves, who have the firstfruits of the Spirit, groan inwardly as we wait eagerly for adoption as sons,* the redemption of our bodies. (ROMANS 8:23)

Related verses: Luke 20:36; John 14:18; Ephesians 1:4–5; Revelation 21:7.

In Romans 8:15, Paul assures you that you have already received the Spirit of adoption as God's child. But in this verse, you eagerly look forward to the full scope of your adoption. Imagine before your Father how your adoption experience will be greatly enriched in heaven.

GOD, YOU WANT ME TO KNOW THAT . . .

YOU WILL ESTABLISH ME ABOVE REPROACH

[Our Lord Jesus Christ] has now reconciled [you] in His body of flesh by His death, in order to present you holy and blameless and above reproach before Him. (COLOSSIANS 1:22)

Related verses: Isaiah 25:8; Zechariah 3:4; Jude 24.

It's hard to comprehend how Jesus Christ could possibly present you *above reproach* before God. Discuss with Him the encouragement and confidence this provides for you.

GOD, YOU WANT ME TO KNOW THAT . . .

I WILL SEE YOU FACE TO FACE

Now we see in a mirror dimly, but then face to face. (1 CORINTHIANS 13:12)

Related verses: Job 19:26–27; 2 Corinthians 4:14; 1 John 3:2; Revelation 22:4.

In Exodus 33:20, Moses was warned by God that no human being could see God's face and live. Recognize before God how Jesus Christ did away with this restriction, and picture what it will be like in heaven to see God face to face.

GOD, YOU WANT ME TO KNOW THAT . . .

I WILL BE WITH YOU

When Christ who is your life appears, then you also will appear with Him in glory. (COLOSSIANS 3:4)

Related verses: John 14:3; 2 Timothy 2:11; Revelation 7:15; 21:3.

On earth, you know God dwells in you according to His promises, but here, you must walk by faith, not by sight (2 Corinthians 5:7). Share with God what you imagine heaven to be like, where you will live and operate freely and openly with Him.

GOD, YOU WANT ME TO KNOW THAT . . .

I WILL ENTER INTO THE JOY OF JESUS

His master said to him, "Well done, good and faithful servant. You have been faithful over a little; I will set you over much. Enter into the joy of your master." (MATTHEW 25:21)

[Jesus said,] "So also you have sorrow now, but *I will see you again, and your hearts will rejoice, and no one will take your joy from you.*" (JOHN 16:22)

Related verses: Psalm 30:5; Isaiah 65:17–19; Jude 24.

What was the most joyful time you can remember? With Jesus, anticipate the joy you will experience when He approaches you warmly with open arms.

66

I Will Live Forever

Much of the Christian experience can be thought of as "already, but not yet." Our experience of life in Christ now is a wonderful foretaste of the glorious life yet to come, but it is only a foretaste. The full extent of eternal life is yet to be experienced—and experience it you will! Everything humanity lost in the fall into sin will be more than fully restored when you enter life eternal. The tree of life in the Garden of Eden, once guarded by an angel with a fiery sword, will be fully accessible to you again. No more weeds, pain, sweat, or danger. Along with new heavens and a new earth, there will be a new you, and that new you will be with the Lord forever!

GOD, YOU WANT ME TO KNOW THAT . . .

YOU WILL ENABLE ME TO EXPERIENCE THE ETERNAL LIFE TO COME

[Jesus said,] "For this is the will of my Father, that everyone who looks on the Son and believes in Him should have eternal life, and I will raise him up on the last day." (JOHN 6:40)

Related verses: Matthew 25:46; Luke 18:30; John 6:51; Romans 6:22; Galatians 6:8; 2 Timothy 1:1; Titus 1:2; 1 John 2:17, 25; Revelation 2:10.

Although you have already passed from death into life by faith in Jesus Christ, imagine for your heavenly Father how the eternal life yet to come will be infinitely richer and more complete.

GOD, YOU WANT ME TO KNOW THAT . . .

YOU WILL RESTORE EDEN FOR ME

[The Lord declares,] "I will make for them a covenant on that day with the beasts of the field, the birds of the heavens, and the creeping things of the ground. And I will abolish the bow, the sword, and war from the land, and I will make you lie down in safety." (HOSEA 2:18)

He who has an ear, let him hear what the Spirit says to the churches. To the one who conquers I will grant to eat of the tree of life, which is in the paradise of God. (REVELATION 2:7)

Related verses: Isaiah 35:9; 65:25; Revelation 7:17; 21:6; 22:1–2, 14, 17.

After Adam and Eve's fall into sin, God graciously blocked their access to the tree of life. Consider the horror of an eternity locked into sin and separated from God. Reflect with the Lord on the significance of you regaining free access to the tree of life in the new heavens and new earth.

GOD, YOU WANT ME TO KNOW THAT . . .

YOU WILL MAKE ME IMMORTAL

The trumpet will sound, and the dead will be raised imperishable, and we shall be changed. For this perishable body must put on the imperishable, and this mortal body must put on immortality. (1 CORINTHIANS 15:52–53)

Related verses: Romans 8:23; 2 Timothy 1:10; Hebrews 9:12.

Ancient mythology and modern fictional superheroes create fantasized immortal beings. Consider with Jesus Christ what it means to you that in Him, you will actually experience immortality.

ALL THINGS MADE NEW

No human mind has ever come close to knowing what is in store for God's beloved. But here are some great previews of the changes to come.

67

The Former Things Will Have Passed Away

Pain, disappointment, broken promises, injuries, hurt feelings, exhaustion—all these have been such a consistent part of your life here in this fallen world that they may almost seem normal. But they are not. They never were a part of God's intent for you. Not only can *you* be frustrated and discouraged by such matters, but creation itself is "groaning" (Romans 8:22), eager for restoration to Eden's perfection and beyond. In heaven, all such "former things" (Revelation 21:4) are gone for good. From the first day in God's kingdom and forever after that, your new life will be joyful, safe, secure, exciting, creative, and satisfying in ways beyond what you could possibly now comprehend.

GOD, YOU WANT ME TO KNOW THAT . . .

THERE WILL BE NO MORE CRYING OR MOURNING

[*God*] *will wipe away every tear from their eyes*, and death shall be no more, *neither shall there be mourning, nor crying*, nor pain anymore, for the former things have passed away. (REVELATION 21:4)

Related verses: Isaiah 35:10; 60:20; 65:19; 2 Thessalonians 2:16–17; Revelation 7:17.

Your Lord sympathizes deeply with your times of mourning, and He keeps all your tears in a bottle (Psalm 56:8). Picture life without sorrowful crying or mourning. Praise God for this future reality.

GOD, YOU WANT ME TO KNOW THAT . . .

THERE WILL BE NO MORE SICKNESS OR PAIN

And no inhabitant will say, "I am sick." (ISAIAH 33:24)

Neither shall there be mourning, nor crying, *nor pain anymore*, for the former things have passed away. (REVELATION 21:4)

Related verses: Malachi 4:2; 2 Thessalonians 1:7.

One terrible consequence of Adam and Eve's fall into sin was the experience of pain, whether through childbirth, strenuous work, sickness, or wounds. Identify for the Lord the significance of you experiencing no more sickness or pain in the life to come.

GOD, YOU WANT ME TO KNOW THAT . . .

YOU WILL MEET MY EVERY NEED

They shall hunger no more, neither thirst anymore; the sun shall not strike them, nor any scorching heat. (REVELATION 7:16)

Related verse: Revelation 14:13.

Here on earth, you experience hunger and thirst, heat and cold, exhaustion and sleep deprivation. Predict for God what life will be like with your every need satisfied.

GOD, YOU WANT ME TO KNOW THAT . . .

YOU WILL MAKE ME SAFE AND SECURE

Behold, the days are coming, declares the LORD, when . . . Judah will be saved, and Israel will dwell securely. (JEREMIAH 23:5–6)

But Israel is saved by the LORD with everlasting salvation; you shall not be put to shame or confounded to all eternity. (ISAIAH 45:17)

Related verses: 1 Chronicles 17:9; Ezekiel 37:26; Joel 3:17; 2 Timothy 2:10; Hebrews 5:9; 9:12; Revelation 21:27; 22:3.

This world, crippled by sin, can be a very dangerous place. There are crime-ridden parts of town, identity thieves and scammers, false friends, and distracted drivers, to name just a few. You constantly need God to save you from your own sin and from the thoughtless and wicked actions of others. Share with your Lord your thoughts and impressions about life in heaven, where you will be completely safe and your residency will be secure forever.

68

I Will Receive My Full Inheritance

When you think of receiving an inheritance, perhaps old movies may come to mind about a room full of relatives waiting to hear the reading of their rich uncle's will and to find out what portion of the estate may be passing to them. Even though God has made it abundantly clear that the inheritance you are to receive, secured through Jesus' sacrifice, is purely a gift of His love, today it might feel almost too wonderful to be true. But in heaven, as Christ's riches are being distributed, there's no question that your name has been plainly called.

GOD, YOU WANT ME TO KNOW THAT . . .

YOU WILL GIVE ME MY INHERITANCE

Therefore [God] is the mediator of a new covenant, so that *those who are called may receive the promised eternal inheritance*, since a death has occurred that redeems them from the transgressions committed under the first covenant. (HEBREWS 9:15)

Then the King will say to those on His right, "Come, you who are blessed by My Father, inherit the kingdom prepared for you from the foundation of the world." (MATTHEW 25:34)

Related verses: Daniel 7:22; Colossians 3:24.

Here you are promised that you will inherit a kingdom, designed and prepared for you from the beginning of time. Those who reject Christ are also promised an inheritance—the eternal fire prepared for the devil and his angels

(Matthew 25:41). Marvel at and glorify God for the undeserved inheritance that awaits you as His beloved child.

GOD, YOU WANT ME TO KNOW THAT . . .

YOU WILL GIVE ME RIGHTEOUSNESS

Wretched man that I am! Who will deliver me from this body of death? Thanks be to God through Jesus Christ our Lord! (ROMANS 7:24–25)

Henceforth there is laid up for me the crown of righteousness, which the Lord, the righteous judge, will award to me on that day, and not only to me but also to all who have loved His appearing. (2 TIMOTHY 4:8)

Related verses: Isaiah 60:21; Jeremiah 23:6; Malachi 4:2; Matthew 5:6; Revelation 3:5.

Of the countless blessings you will enjoy in heaven, perhaps the crowning blessing will be that God sets you free from your old sinful nature. You will be perfectly righteous there. Discuss the significance of this remarkable truth with your Lord Jesus Christ.

69

The Glory of the Lord Will Be Revealed

You are going to shine in glory forever. Yes, you! And every one of your fellow believers will marvel at what God has done in and through you. You are to reign with your Lord Jesus Christ forever! The day of your complete salvation is indeed closer now than it was on the day you first believed. As previously noted, it could be today!

GOD, YOU WANT ME TO KNOW THAT . . .

I WILL WITNESS YOUR UNIMAGINABLE GLORY

***The glory of the LORD shall be revealed, and all flesh shall see it together,* for the mouth of the LORD has spoken.** (ISAIAH 40:5)

Related verses: 1 Chronicles 29:11; Romans 5:2; 1 Corinthians 2:9–10; 1 Peter 5:1.

In this life, you have been privileged to witness glimpses of God's glory—in the complexity and majesty of creation, in the power of God's Word in transforming lives, and through God's mercy, grace, and love in your life. Express to the Lord what you think it will be like to fully experience His incomparable glory and majesty.

GOD, YOU WANT ME TO KNOW THAT . . .

I WILL EXPERIENCE YOUR EVERLASTING LIGHT

The sun shall be no more your light by day, nor for brightness shall the moon give you light; but the LORD will be your everlasting light, and your God will be your glory. (ISAIAH 60:19)

Related verses: Psalm 36:9; Revelation 21:23; 22:5.

The sun's light, essential to life on earth, will be infinitely upgraded to the Sun of Righteousness (Malachi 4:2), Jesus Christ Himself. Imagine before the Lord this entirely new way of seeing in heaven.

GOD, YOU WANT ME TO KNOW THAT . . .

YOUR SON WILL BE GLORIFIED IN ME

[*Jesus*] *comes on that day to be glorified in His saints*, and to be marveled at among all who have believed, because our testimony to you was believed. (2 THESSALONIANS 1:10)

Related verse: Isaiah 44:23.

God is indeed glorified in His marvelous creation, in His superlative attributes, and in His absolute goodness and perfection. But consider the amazing fact that in heaven for all eternity, Jesus will be glorified first and foremost *in you*, whom God has lovingly made His own child. Present your thoughts to Him about this marvelous truth.

GOD, YOU WANT ME TO KNOW THAT . . .

YOU WILL GLORIFY ME

To this [God] called you through our gospel, so that *you may obtain the glory of our Lord Jesus Christ.* (2 THESSALONIANS 2:14)

Related verses: Isaiah 62:2; Daniel 12:3; Zechariah 9:16; Matthew 13:43; 1 Peter 5:4.

In the related verses above, your glory in heaven is compared to the shining sun and stars, the brightness of the sky, and jewels in a crown. Picture for God yourself and your fellow believers in this way.

GOD, YOU WANT ME TO KNOW THAT . . .

I WILL REIGN WITH YOU FOREVER

Night will be no more. They will need no light of lamp or sun, for the Lord God will be their light, and *they will reign forever and ever.* (REVELATION 22:5)

Related verses: 1 Corinthians 6:2–3; 2 Timothy 2:12; Revelation 3:21.

What an unexpected kingdom God has prepared for you! His objective is not to dominate you but to reign with you. Meditate richly before the Lord God about what your role and position in heaven will be.

YOUR TRIP SUMMARY

70

The Coming Ages

Jesus Christ is indeed the same yesterday, today, and forever. You did not choose God, but He chose you. Before creation, God established His plan to love you and save you from your sins. He brought you to Himself, He created faith in your heart, and He has given you new life and has exalted you. My prayer is that throughout your life, you will continue to explore and savor all that God in Christ has done for you, continues to do today, and promises to do throughout all eternity. God is faithful, and He will bring it to pass. And in Christ, all of His promises to you are most assuredly yes!

> **But God, being rich in mercy, because of the great love with which He loved us, even when we were dead in our trespasses, made us alive together with Christ—by grace you have been saved—and raised us up with Him and seated us with Him in the heavenly places in Christ Jesus, so that in the coming ages He might show the immeasurable riches of His grace in kindness toward us in Christ Jesus.** (EPHESIANS 2:4–7)
>
> **The Spirit and the Bride say, "Come." And let the one who hears say, "Come." And let the one who is thirsty come; let the one who desires take the water of life without price. . . . He who testifies to these things says, "Surely I am coming soon." Amen. Come, Lord Jesus!** (REVELATION 22:17, 20)

Recall several promises and assurances that have been reinforced or magnified for you through your journey in

this book. Thank God for all His amazing promises and assurances!

NAMES OF GOD

There is only one true God, as revealed in the Bible: "Hear, O Israel: The LORD our God, the LORD is one" (Deuteronomy 6:4).

But that one God reveals Himself as three distinct persons: Father, Son, and Holy Spirit (Matthew 28:19).

To express this great mystery, the term *Trinity* was chosen. This diagram organizes names, titles, and descriptions of God from the Bible verses quoted in this book.

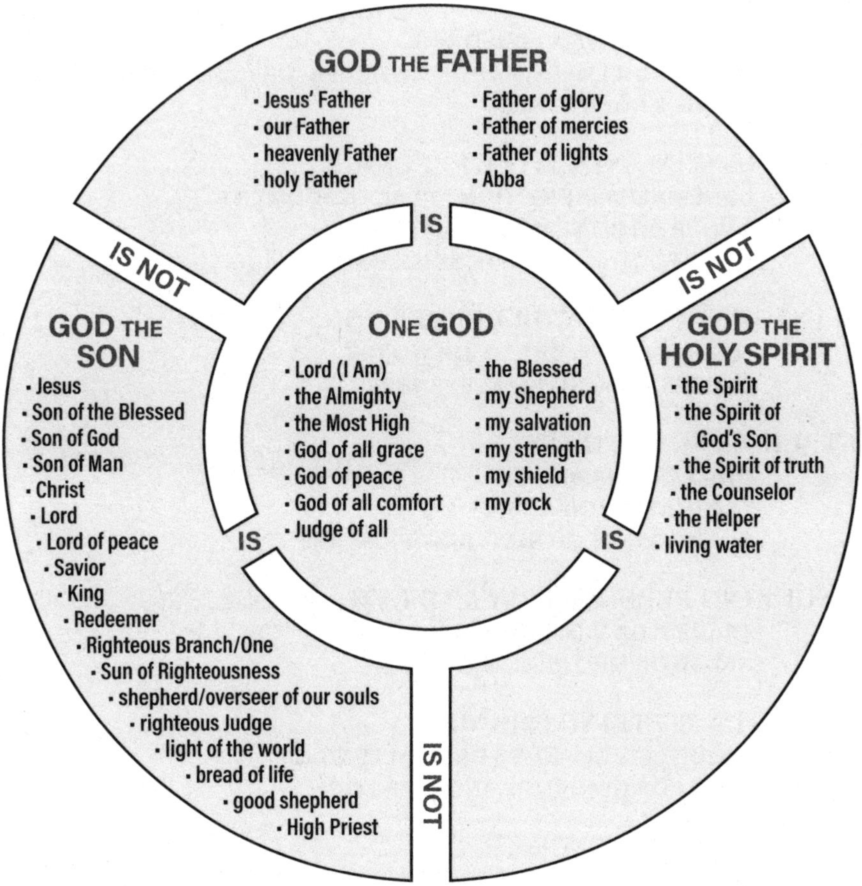

PROMISES FOR DIFFICULT TIMES

Inherited mental vulnerabilities and experienced traumatic events are all too common in our broken world. Medication and counseling can certainly be helpful—even the apostle Paul took Luke, the "beloved physician" (Colossians 4:14), along with him on his missionary journeys. But God's Word is always appropriate and effective for every aspect of your life. Following are recommended readings for various challenges that you might be facing.

IF YOU ARE . . .

Grieving a Loss

GRIEF, LOSS OF A LOVED ONE

PHYSICAL ILLNESS, PAIN, HANDICAPS, OR LIMITATIONS

AGING, END OF LIFE

Experiencing Negative Feelings

LONELINESS, REJECTION, OR ABANDONMENT

ANGER OR BITTERNESS

DISAPPOINTMENT OR RESENTMENT

Managing Anxiety or Depression

FEAR, ANXIETY, DREAD, OR WORRY

DEPRESSION OR HOPELESSNESS

Struggling with Sin

GUILT OR SHAME

TEMPTATION OR ADDICTION

COMPROMISE OR SELF-JUSTIFICATION

Enduring Persecution and Evil

TRAUMA OR VIOLENCE

ABUSE OR MISTREATMENT

Facing Unsettling Change

MAJOR LIFE CHANGES OR CHALLENGES

NEED FOR GUIDANCE AND DIRECTION

Lacking Confidence

DOUBT OR UNCERTAINTY

FEELINGS OF INADEQUACY

WORTHLESSNESS OR LACK OF PURPOSE